# JOHN PAUL II

VALENTINA ALAZRAKI
SLAWOMIR ODER

# John Paul II

*The Saint Who Conquered
the Heart of the World*

Translated by Luis Berrios

ST PAULS

First published in Mexico in 2014 under the title *Juan Pablo II: El santo que conquistó el corazón del mundo* by PLANETA MEXICO – Mexico.

English language edition © 2014 by the Society of St. Paul

English translation by Luis Berrios


Library of Congress Cataloging-in-Publication Data

Alazraki, Valentina, 1955- author.
　[Juan Pablo II. English]
　John Paul II: the saint who conquered the heart of the world / Valentina Alazraki, Slawomir Oder.
　　pages cm
　First published in Mexico in 2014 under the title Juan Pablo II: El santo que conquistó el corazón del mundo by Planeta Mexico. English translation by Luis Berrios.
　ISBN 978-0-8189-1372-3
　1. John Paul II, Pope, 1920-2005. 2. Popes—Biography. I. Oder, Slawomir, 1960- author. II. Alazraki, Valentina, 1955- Juan Pablo II. Translation of: III. Title.
　BX1378.5A354513 2014
　282.092—dc23
　[B]

2014020775


Produced and designed in the United States of America by the
Fathers and Brothers of the Society of St. Paul,
2187 Victory Boulevard, Staten Island, New York 10314-6603
as part of their communications apostolate.


ISBN 978-0-8189-1372-3

Current Printing - first digit　　1　　2　　3　　4　　5　　6　　7　　8　　9　　1 0

Place of Publication:
2187 Victory Blvd., Staten Island, NY 10314 - USA


Year of Current Printing - first year shown

2014　　2015　　2016　　2017　　2018　　2019　　2020　　2021　　2022　　2023

To my parents Theresa and Romuald, who taught me to believe, to love, and to hope.

*Slawomir Oder*


"He who lives among us never dies."

*Valentina Alazraki*

# Table of Contents

# Introduction

This book was born as a result of our having been privileged witnesses to one of the longest pontificates in the history of the Catholic Church. For almost 27 years, and from a variety of perspectives, ecclesiastical and journalistic, we have been participating witnesses in the development of one of the most influential leaderships in the twentieth century.

From the conclave that announced Karol Wojtyla as the Vicar of Christ to the world; his pilgrimages throughout the world; the assassination attempt that nearly cost him his life; the illness that gradually eroded his health, but not his mission; his death; the process of his beatification and now canonization, the name of John Paul II has always been present in all areas of our daily lives.

This is why we decided to write this story, with four hands and as one narrator, which is our witness to the invaluable legacy of the man who lived constantly in the service of others. Textual quotes were used only when strictly needed in order to avoid losing precision in the story.

The canonization of John Paul II is the starting point to remind future generations of the unsurpassable and charismatic spirit that characterized the Pope who changed the world. Here are our voices, anecdotes, and experiences that collectively are intended to deliver a biographical accounting of the Pope who is now a saint.

Here both Valentina Alazraki the journalist, and I, Monsignor Slawomir Oder, the postulator of the cause to canonize John Paul II, speak.

*Valentina Alazraki*
*Slawomir Oder*

# 1   The Sanctity of John Paul II

After his election on October 16, 1978, Karol Wojtyla would begin a life under spotlights that would never go out, not even following his death; they continue to light his path, first towards beatification, and then towards canonization and beyond.

From the moment that he appeared in the central loggia of St. Peter's Basilica to greet and speak extemporaneously to the crowd, and in doing so breaking a protocol of centuries even though he had been forewarned that he could only appear to impart the blessing, we all understood that John Paul II, "whom the cardinals had chosen from a distant country" as he referred to himself, would be an atypical Pope. He would be a strong figure, full of energy, with a projection and charisma that would without a doubt leave a profound impression on history.

From that day on he decided to become a missionary, and follow in St. Paul's footsteps. He understood that his parish was the entire world, a world without borders, and that he had to exercise a universal paternity. To that end he utilized his attributes: his knowledge of multiple languages, his youth, his sympathy, and his extraordinary skills as communicator. He put them to use to fulfill his mission.

For twenty-six and a half years he was a man of the masses,

someone who, especially during the first years of his pontificate constantly broke with protocol to get closer to the people, to shake hands, to carry children in his arms, and in doing so drove his security detail crazy. One could make a book of photographs with John Paul II's outstretched hands towards the people, in all contexts and every continent.

After the assassination attempt on May 13, 1981, with the only purpose of silencing his prophetic voice, John Paul II continued to be a man of action. His mysticism, devotion to the Virgin Mary and Divine Providence, as well as his acceptance of the cross as the foundation of his service, became more and more evident.

Monsignor Alfred Xuereb (one of John Paul II's collaborators who was prelate of the Antechamber during his pontificate's final years and who would later become Pope Benedict XVI's second secretary and is now one of Pope Francis' secretaries) warned on many occasions that John Paul II had the conviction that Divine Providence had granted him the possibility of living a second life and that, in response to such a gift, he had to offer himself to the service of others until the end.

John Paul II liked to be among people, but he also enjoyed being in solitude. He loved to escape from the Vatican to go to the mountains and walk in his sports shoes, stop to talk to a peasant or families on excursion, read the breviary while contemplating the mountains, eat a snack prepared by a policeman's wife, sleep under a tree, or recite the Liturgy of the Hours near a waterfall.

Those in charge of his security, who accompanied him in his "off program" excursions throughout the years, cherish an inerasable memory of the most intimate and human side of John Paul II that never ceased to be present, despite being the most charismatic and acclaimed Pope in history. John Paul II was also a very wise man, who knew how to "read" the world in a very intelligent manner, fought to defeat oppressive systems, and condemned dictatorships and mafias alike.

He never ceased to surprise the world with his intuitions and gestures. He understood that young people are the future of society and the Church and that, without them, both would be sterile. He was the man who convened the extraordinary Jubilee of 2000, because the day of his election, Cardinal Wyszynski prophesied to him that he would lead mankind into the third millennium.

He wrote fourteen encyclicals, but the principal one was the one he wrote with suffering and the cross upon his shoulders. Perhaps the most eloquent image of his entire pontificate is one of his last, when on Good Friday he followed the Via Crucis from his private chapel, embracing a crucifix to share his own Calvary with Jesus Christ. During his entire pontificate and the years following his death, the world wondered about the secret to his charm, the essence of his sanctity, that the Church has now recognized officially. John Paul II was a shepherd who, like Pope Francis would say, "smelled like his sheep" because he immersed himself in the middle of the herd.

The most outstanding revelation during the beatification and canonization process was that no unknown aspects or major surprises of the Polish Pope were found. The process put into evidence his entire life in total transparency. There was not a public and a private Wojtyla. His gestures both as a man and as a priest were transparent from the beginning of his youth until his death. The world knew him exactly as he was; witnessed his sympathy, his fervor in prayer, his spontaneity, his capacity to establish human relationships marked by his warmth and simplicity. There were no surprises because he lived with extraordinary transparency.

He shared with all of us like a father with his family. Being a totally coherent man, with harmony between his thoughts and his actions, he maintained his clarity even during his illness. Even though he drooled, could neither speak nor move, he continued to be himself, with all of his burden of humanity and love of Christ.

The profound and serious way with which he lived his life was surprising. He was a happy, accomplished, and complete man. The synthesis of his life was to live a normal life in an extraordinary and full way. He lived his priesthood and his humanity completely and fully.

John Paul II used to say that his first learning experience was actually at home, with his father. It was not until he was 22 years of age that he became aware that "his journey" would have to take him through the seminary in Cracow. It became an event that, as he reiterated on many occasions "continued to be a mystery":

> How is it possible to explain the ways of the Lord? What I do know is that in a determined moment in my life, I was certain that Christ told me what He had told thousands of others before me: "Come and follow Me."

# 2   Priest, Bishop, Cardinal, Pope

When Pope Paul VI passed away on August 6, 1978, Cardinal Wojtyla, while speaking with friends, outlined a prophetic description of the future needs of the Church: "I believe that the Church as well as the entire world needs a very spiritual Pope. This will have to be his first and most indispensable characteristic in order to be a good parent. Asia, Africa and Latin America are living through very problematic situations and will look to Pope Paul VI's successor to help them, but most importantly, to understand them."

Cardinal Wojtyla was delighted with the election of John Paul I. He added: "I believe that he is the ideal choice, because of his piety and humility, to listen to the Holy Spirit. He is the Pope that the Church needs today." Thirty-three days later, on the evening of September 28, 1978, John Paul I passed away.

On October 16, at 5:15 P.M., John Paul II emerged from the conclave elected as the 264th Pope. He was the first non-Italian Pope after Adrian VI from Holland who was elected in 1522. When he was asked if he accepted the mandate, he responded that "he accepted in obedience to the faith, before Christ his Lord, abandoning himself to the Mother of Christ and the Church, being aware of the great difficulties that lay ahead."

The most striking element of his beatification and canonization process was the discovery and confirmation of the source of his coherence, energy, enthusiasm, depth and natural ease. This source, according to more than one hundred witnesses interviewed during the process, was his encounter with Christ, to be in love with Christ, and to feel loved by Christ.

Much has been written about his life, including his own books, speeches, and autobiographical memoirs. However, on one occasion he revealed something very intimate: "Everyone tries to understand me by my exterior, but I can only be understood by what's inside of me."

Among the pieces that constitute the mosaic of his sanctity, both his gift and joy in prayer that accompanied him since he was a child until his final hours, emerge very strongly.

## Prayer

To John Paul II, prayer represented a daily pilgrimage to the source of life itself, which to him was Jesus Christ. Thirteen days after his election, the Pope went with some of his collaborators to the Shrine of Our Lady of Mentorella near Rome, which he used to visit regularly when he was Cardinal. During his visit he asked his travel companions: "What is more important to the Pope in his life, in his work?" Everyone tried to answer but none of them hit the mark. John Paul II responded that prayer was most important to him because, he explained, from prayer emerges the capacity to tell the truth without fear, "since whomever finds himself alone before Christ does not fear man."

When one of his best friends, Polish Cardinal Andrzej Maria Deskur, was paralyzed as a result of an ictus or stroke, and was forced to resign his position at the Vatican, he wrote him a letter that read: "Now you know what your mission in the Church is. It was about the mission of prayer, of caring for the sick and all who suffer." "That letter" – recalled Cardinal Deskur – "helped me tremendously."

During difficult moments in his ministry, or those that were especially critical, John Paul II sought direction through prayer. When his collaborators, whom he had asked for possible solutions to any given problem, recognized not having found a solution, John Paul II, very serenely and confidently would tell them: "Don't worry, we will find it after we pray a little more." During a particularly dramatic circumstance, the Pope intoned the *Miserere* loudly.

Prayer marked his life. He would enter the chapel at 5:00 A.M., where he prayed until 6:00 A.M. He would later retire to his living quarters to meditate, and then return to the chapel at 7:00 A.M. to celebrate Mass. Each morning he recited the consecration to the Sacred Heart: on a piece of paper that had turned yellow and that he had folded like a scapular, John Paul II had written: "All for you, Most Sacred Heart of Jesus." His collaborators described him as a man of "heroic prayer."

He felt a special veneration for the saints. Each morning after breakfast he used to walk across the sacristy and kiss all relics that stood on a small table next to the altar. Next to a relic from Christ's True Cross, there were reliquaries with pieces of remains from St. Peter, St. Stanislaw, St. Charles Borromeo, St. Jadwiga, and of numerous Blesseds and Saints. In his later years, when he went about in his wheelchair, he would ask to be taken to where the reliquaries were so he could continue to venerate them. During his pontificate, and with the purpose of offering the faithful a wide repertoire of role models to imitate, he proclaimed 483 Saints and 1,345 Blesseds. He kept two thick binders in his room, which contained the biographies of all of them, which he would read frequently to become inspired in the practice of the virtues. This heroic exercise would lead him to beatification and sanctification.

Prayer was the air he breathed, the water he drank, the food that nourished him. It was an expression of his own Christian and priestly identity. On one occasion in the Roman Seminary, one of the seminarians asked him what it meant to him to be Christ's Vicar. He responded that before he became Christ's Vicar, "he was a priest that acted *in persona Christi*." To him being a priest represented the heart of his identity, the fixing of his being "in God's image." To him, a priest had to be a man of God before anything, who represented for the faithful a witness to absolute and invisible realities; a man of prayer; a teacher; a mentor and a friend. His faith was based upon this conviction, and throughout his life he never ceased to be, above all, a priest.

There were no whimsy or dark moments in John Paul II's life, no zones without God. He made God permeate his entire existence which he lived as a continuous dialogue with the Lord. Early on in his youth he answered the call that Christ made to him, a call to share His cross. Through the challenges he faced, his was a positive and daily response to that call. In that sense, and since he was convinced that his relationship with others passed through Christ because Christ was present in every encounter, John Paul II was a mystic.

Many witnesses interviewed during the beatification process qualified John Paul II as a "man of prayer." His desire for perfection, in other words to be in God's presence, found its maximum expression during his lifetime of prayer. He seemed to always be in God's presence and always sought to find life's spiritual perfection at all times. He spent many hours in prayer;

he had great confidence in the Lord's mercy. His faith impressed everyone; he was a role model to follow.

His ability and spontaneity to shift from being in contact with multitudes of people to the solace of being in an intimate colloquium with God were impressive. When in prayer, nothing that was occurring in his surroundings seemed to bother him. To his collaborators, it was a great mystery how he could reconcile his multiple commitments with such an intense life of prayer. He simply shifted from work to prayer. He had an extraordinary gift to extract from prayer the strength and energy to remain active all day.

His love of Jesus, just as his desire to submerge himself in His passion, made him love the Via Crucis with predilection. Every Friday, whether it was during his travels or in the Vatican, he made the fourteen Stations of the Cross. In the Vatican, he did it either in his chapel or terrace where representations of the fourteen pictures of the Way to Calvary had been placed. Because there are no stations in Castel Gandolfo, he prayed in a hallway where a set of lithographs about the painful Way to Calvary had been placed.

When he lived in Poland, Karol Wojtyla loved the sanctuary of Kalwaria Zebrzydowska dearly. He visited even when the road was covered with snow or mud. For this reason he always carried a pair of boots in his car. He used to pray the Via Crucis and would take from three to four hours. He himself indicated that on one occasion while making the Via Crucis, he solved many pastoral issues.

His spokesperson Joaquin Navarro Valls, narrated that on Friday April 1, 2005, a day before his death, John Paul II's clinical diagnosis was very grave. Around ten o'clock in the morning, they noticed that he wanted to tell them something, but could not understand him. Sister Tobiana gave him a pencil and a sheet of paper, and he wrote that he wanted to pray the Via Crucis. She read the fourteen stations to him and he, with great effort, would cross himself to begin each station.

He would also express his love for God in his desire to please Him by converting the hearts of those people he encountered, and who for some reason had become distant from Him. Nurse Rita Megliorim, who cared for him at the Gemelli Hospital, mentioned that John Paul II asked that images of both the Virgin of Czestochowa and the Merciful Jesus be placed in front of his bed. One evening, while he was apparently asleep, the nurse was very tired, and rested her arms and head on the Pope's bed and fell half asleep. Suddenly, she felt the pontiff's hand over her cheek and noticed that he looked intensely at the Virgin's painting. The Pope said nothing, but she had the feeling that he was entrusting her to the Virgin. It was a very intense and overwhelming experience because she felt that they were in another dimension.

According to his personal physician, Dr. Renato Buzzonetti, he very rarely refrained from receiving the Eucharist or celebrating Mass, even when he was ill. John Paul II, he added, followed the advice he was given but on his own terms in the sense that, if he had a fever and was instructed to stay in his room, he did not stop going to the chapel to pray, even if this was against medical advice.

John Paul II's love of God was evident throughout his entire life. In Poland, and during his pontificate, it was common to find him lying on the floor before the tabernacle praying. Mother Tobiana, who cared for him day and night in the Vatican with extraordinary dedication, especially during the last years of his life, indicated that John Paul II always lived in unity with

Christ. He spoke to Him about the world's salvation constantly and to have mercy on everyone. In his daily prayer he included the continents, countries and cities. He visited nunciatures, bishoprics, seminaries, monasteries, jails, hospitals, orphanages, departments of the curia, and the families all over the world. He was always in contemplation and listening to God.

On one occasion John Paul II narrated that he used to receive hundreds of letters with prayer intentions and that he kept them in his chapel to always have them present in his consciousness, even if he could not read them every day. He left them for Jesus. "Those intentions are always in my heart," he said.

The Pope prayed quite a bit for the deceased. He used to mention the names of cardinals, bishops, friends, and relatives of his collaborators who had passed away. All who concelebrated Mass with him, attended a private Mass at which he officiated, or simply saw him pray, agree that he prayed with great intensity, and that is how he truly came in direct contact with God. Everyone, including those who were not Catholic, commented that they saw something supernatural in him, and felt stimulated by a stronger spirituality.

At night, when he could not sleep he prayed. When he was still able to walk, he would come out of the apostolic department's terrace, kneel on the floor, lean against the wall and pray. He would go to his chapel and pray for extended periods of time before his audiences. As he walked by a cross located in his terrace, he always kissed it.

The manner in which he prepared to celebrate Mass was extraordinary. He never missed one. The night before, he would recite the prayers for next day's Mass in Latin and remember the intentions for which and/or for whom he had celebrated the previous one. During their testimonies, his classmates at the

Belgian College in Rome, where Wojtyla studied between 1946 and 1948, recalled that when they saw him pray, they felt as if they were pagans recently converted. According to them, he was naturally open to transcendence.

One of his former Masters of Ceremonies, Monsignor Piero Marini, told us that on one occasion during his visit to Pordenone in May of 1992, and before the celebration of Mass, the Pope went to the rest-room. When he noticed that the Pope did not return, and concerned about a possible delay to the program, he went looking for him. Through a semi-open door he saw that the Pope, leaning against a sink, was kneeling and praying.

Similar scenes were lived and witnessed throughout the world. Papal trip organizers always tried to make sure that during a visit to a religious residence or institution, John Paul II did not walk by a chapel. They were always concerned that he would enter and begin to pray, which would mean a delay to a program of activities that was already fully loaded. The same took place in any churches he visited. He would kneel before the main altar and no one could approach him to alert him that time was pressing. To him this was not a waste of time, but a way to become energized to find the best way to carry out his commitments.

We were all witness of how, despite his physical limitations, the Pope always wanted to kneel, especially before the Blessed Sacrament; in his youth he would actually prostrate himself on the floor, and there nuns would find him after several hours in prayer.

The chapel was the most important place in any of his residences, his truly vital place, and the central enclosure. He entered it when he woke, and returned to it several times a day. When he had to make an important decision, he spent a few moments there. There was a small table inside the chapel of the Palace of the Archbishop of Cracow, where he wrote the most important documents.

His recollection was visibly different from all of the others. Several of his collaborators commented that on occasions when he was alone in the chapel, they could hear voices, as if he was carrying a conversation with someone.

After the May 13, 1981 assassination attempt, and after six hours in surgery and an extended period of time in intensive care, he woke up as if nothing had happened, and asked his secretary Stanislaw Dziwisz: "Have we prayed *complines* already?" All nuncios who received him on his world travels narrated that on different circumstances after returning from exhausting journeys, he would retire to the chapel to thank God for everything he had been able to accomplish that day. On many occasions and right after waking the next morning, the nuncios would find him already in the chapel. Sometimes he never even slept.

The Mexican nuncio, Monsignor Justo Mullor, narrated that during his fourth visit to Mexico in 1999, after that unforgettable encounter with multiple generations of Mexicans in the Aztec Stadium, John Paul II returned to the nunciature full of joy. The Pope commented to him that seeing children, young people and the elderly together gave him a marvelous synthesis of what Mexico was about. That same evening, the Pope went to bed early, but towards eleven o'clock he got up and went to the chapel, where he remained until six o'clock in the morning. The Pope's secretary commented to Monsignor Mullor that he had been praying all night to thank God for having been able to deliver the post-synodal exhortation for the Synod of America.

All physicians and nurses who cared for him during his multiple stays at the Gemelli Hospital have commented that

John Paul II would get up at five in the morning and begin to pray. At seven in the morning he celebrated or assisted at the celebration of Mass by his secretary, would read the breviary, or pray the rosary during the day. On Sundays, and despite his precarious health, he would ask to be taken to the chapel on his floor, the tenth, to pray the *Angelus*. During his hospital stay after fracturing his right femur, he remained awake the evening between May 17 and 18, his birthday, to thank God and his mother for having been born. He felt that he owed them that sacrifice.

## Eucharist

Another piece of his sanctity's mosaic was certainly his relationship with the Eucharist, which he put at the center of his life. He was primarily a priest who always participated in the ministry of faith, and the death and resurrection of Jesus Christ.

During the *Angelus* of September 4, 2005 in Castel Gandolfo, Benedict XVI recalled:

> John Paul II celebrated Mass with great devotion, the center of every one of his days, and how much time he spent in quiet and adoring prayer before the Most High. During the final months of his life, his illness made him to resemble the suffering Jesus even more. It was moving to think that in his final hour, the offering of his own life and that of Christ joined together in the holy Mass that was taking place by his bedside.

His sanctity highlights the normality of a vocation that has the Eucharistic sacrifice as its center, the capacity to see God's presence in everyone and everything, and the conviction that life is a debt of love. He speaks of sanctity as a duty of justice, because in Christ, man is called upon to be whole. By participating in Christ's sacrifice, man returns to God what he has received. Full justice is achieved when man responds totally with sanctity; it is for this reason that to John Paul II, sanctity that passes through the Eucharist is a duty of justice.

Indeed, his entire life highlights the awareness of being a debtor. He had the certainty that there were people who suffered in his place. For example, his relationship with the Jewish people on one hand reflected his vision that all men are in God's image; on the other hand, his awareness that the Jewish people – including friends of his – had suffered. He felt that a debt had to be paid for that suffering.

According to many of his collaborators, his humility was noticeably extraordinary during his Eucharistic celebrations, which he presented before God as a humble servant. To John Paul II, the Eucharist was the most important moment of his day. From it, he extracted the strength to carry out his mission. Before and after the Eucharistic celebrations, he remained in prayer for more than fifteen minutes, as a way of giving thanks. It was amazing to assist to these moments of prayer because it gave the impression that he was not present but in another dimension. It seemed that before addressing the people, John Paul II spoke with God. Before representing Him, he asked to be His living image among men.

He demonstrated his great love for the Eucharist in the celebration of *Corpus Christi* (the solemnity of Christ's Body and Blood). When he was the Archbishop of Cracow, he became upset when the communist authorities did not allow the procession to march through the center of the city, but the following Sunday they allowed a dog parade. To him this was an insult to the Lord.

After his election as Pope he decided that to celebrate *Corpus Christi* a procession would take place from the Basilica of St. John Lateran, where he celebrated Mass, to the Basilica of St. Mary Major. On one occasion during the last years of his life, during the procession that he made in a special vehicle and despite his physical limitations, he tried to kneel before the Most High. Both his secretary and master of ceremonies knew that he should not do it because his knees could no longer support his weight. Additionally, knowing of the instability of his body in general, it was dangerous because of the vehicle's movement. The Pope however, insisted. His master of ceremonies commented that due to his insistence they helped him to kneel, but immediately noticed that he could not sustain that position, and had to help him back to his seat while enduring great suffering.

The Pope even dedicated an entire year to the Eucharist, and this was the theme of his last encyclical, *Ecclesia de eucharistia;* additionally, he instituted the Perpetual Adoration at St. Peter's Basilica. The Pope's life had a profound and radical Eucharistic sense, which gave his personality an irresistible charm. By being an authentic man, truly committed to his sacramental life, the pontiff could establish and propose high goals to men whose potential, sometimes hidden, derived from being children of God, redeemed by Christ, who loved them until the end, called them to communion with the Lord and a life of sanctity.

I remember my first encounter with the Holy Father, when I participated in the congress that took place in Czestochowa on June 18, 1983. It was one of those encounters that, by entering your life suddenly and forcefully, breaks it apart, planting a seed of restlessness where you cannot pretend that nothing happened, and that your life continued as before. Even after that first moment of enthusiasm, when you try to return to normalcy, trying to archive that encounter among others already lived, that seed that had been cast remains hidden, only to emerge at the right moment with all its strength of conviction and restlessness, defying you to face the challenge with courage.                         *Monsignor Slawomir Oder*

The awareness of the gift received constantly transformed John Paul II's life, marked by the urgency to be grateful to God. In his book *Gift and Mystery*, he wrote that in the Eucharist, Christ gives everything He received back to the Father. John Paul II paid his debt with enthusiasm and tireless work, always announcing, in all latitudes, Christ's solidarity with each individual, each generation, which converges in the guarantee of dignity for each human being.

The Pope convinced the faithful that Christ loves them to the point that He sacrificed Himself for them, and that love strengthens. His love was such, that in the last years of his life, when his physical strength had abandoned him, the pontiff drew strength from within because of the conviction of that love. He believed that when he celebrated the Eucharist, he did so *in persona Christi*, and that conviction dominated his life. He never stopped feeling that he was elected from among the others to bring man closer to God, and God closer to man.

## Mary

A very special aspect of his spirituality was his relationship with Mary. John Paul II's religiosity could be summarized with the motto of his pontificate, *Totus tuus* (all yours), because he saw everything through his Mother the Virgin Mary's eyes, and that of the Church.

The most mature fruit of his human and Christian richness was really seen when, forty days before his death, after having undergone a tracheotomy, after waking up and being unable to speak, he wrote on a board: "What have they done to me?... *Totus tuus.*" In his intimate encounters with God, the figure of Mary always occupied a privileged place. His relationship with her, was demonstrated not only through prayer, but also in his daily activities and evident artistic sensibility.

His speeches always contained references to Louis Grignion de Montfort's prayer: *Totus tuus ego sum et omnia mea tua sunt* ("I and all that is mine is yours"). His preferred prayer was the rosary; he always carried it in his pocket and there was always one on his night table.

During the month of May, he sang litanies to the Virgin of Fatima on his terrace every day, before a statue of her that was placed in a small altar. He introduced the "prayer of the humble" in the rosary, a series of five mysteries of light relative to the key moments of Jesus' public life, and he dedicated a special year to Mary.

Mary was present in each of Karol Wojtyla's life events. She was like a star that guided his footsteps. She had a direct or indirect influence over his decisions, his nature, and his relationship with others. His total consecration to Mary represented a passage to the mature and conscientious phase of his faith. Frequently, the Marian dimension of his spirituality was related to the dramatic events of his childhood, when he lost his mother at a very early age. His spirituality however, took shape in a profoundly virile climate, since his first teacher of the faith was his father, Karol Wojtyla, a military man with a totally unblemished faith. It was his father who instilled in him the profound devotion to the Holy Spirit and St. Joseph. He accompanied him to the Kalwaria Zebrzydowska Sanctuary in Czestochowa, and initiated him in the traditional Marian piety of the Polish people.

He was a member of the Marian Congregation during his youth, of which he even became president. The activities within this group contributed to developing young Karol's Marian devotion.

His relationship with Mary intensified strongly and profoundly during Poland's Nazi occupation, which coincided with his juvenile years, his Christian and humane maturation, his struggle to survive and the awakening of his vocation.

It was in this phase that Jan Tyranowski, a humble tailor, performed a very important role. He was a layman with a very profound faith, who served as spiritual guide for many young people. It was he who introduced Karol to Louis Grignion's treatise on *True Devotion to the Virgin Mary*, while he worked in the quarries. Additionally, he organized a "living rosary" prayer group, through which he encouraged young people to deepen their faith.

The encounter with Tyranowski was pivotal in Karol's life because it not only helped him deepen in his faith and establish a more personal relationship with God, but to discover his vocation to the priesthood.

His maturation in the faith and true devotion to the Virgin, which culminated in his consecration, were truly solidified with his decision to enter the seminary. He decided to follow the path of priesthood shortly after his twentieth birthday, and despite the strong persecution the Church was enduring, he firmly believed and trusted in Divine help.

Those who knew him in his youth believe that the loneliness that he experienced after his father's death provoked that introspective young man to feel the need for an individual and personal relationship with God. Certainly his devotion to Mary facilitated that journey.

On one occasion John Paul II was asked if he had ever seen the Virgin. He replied: "I have not seen her but I can hear her."

During his last trip to Poland, one of his collaborators met him in the small chapel where the Virgin of Czestochowa is located. He had to kneel very close to the pontiff and realized that at some point while he prayed, he spoke loudly. "I am not sure what they were saying to each other, but it was an exceptional colloquium. It appeared that it was never going to end and although it delayed the program considerably, it was an extraordinary experience for me."

There is a phrase that John Paul II uttered after the fall of the Berlin Wall that reflects his absolute confidence in the Virgin: "She has done her part, it is now our turn to do ours." John Paul II wanted to restore the veneration of God's Mother in the Church. He was convinced that the new evangelization had to go through her, and therefore through all the Marian sanctuaries that were a mandatory stop for him during his pilgrimages throughout the world.

He firmly believed that those sanctuaries represented a great capital for the Church, because they are places where pilgrims' experiences intertwine with the mystery of Mary, and where the experiences of a nation, of a country, of a region, encounter the love of the Church and her Mother.

It is no coincidence that the first objective of his first visit as pontiff was a Marian sanctuary; that of the Virgin of Guadalupe.

## Guadalupe

John Paul II was a devotee of the Virgin of Guadalupe, even before he visited Mexico. He himself explained it on the eve of his first international trip:

> I too come from a nation and land whose heart beats within the great Marian Sanctuaries. This allows me to understand the people, the Church, and the continent whose heart beats in the Sanctuary of the Mother of God, of Guadalupe.

During his last general audience before departing to Mexico on January 25, 1978, the Pope demonstrated his hope that "The Morenita" might open "a path to the heart of that Church, their people and continent."

This catechesis was in some way John Paul II's first declaration of love towards Mexico, who even before embarking on his first trip had understood that his approach to the country with the second largest number of Catholics in Latin America would be accomplished through devotion to the Virgin of Guadalupe.

The next day, during the farewell ceremony at the Fiumicino Airport, he said once more:

> The Pope will prostrate himself before the prodigious image of Mexico's Virgin of Guadalupe to invoke her maternal help and protection over the papal ministry itself; to repeat with increased strength for his new and immense obligations "I am all yours"; to put the principle of his pontificate, and the future of the continent's evangelization in her hands.

While he was aboard the plane that took him to Mexico, he said that the greatest hope he had during this trip was to

kneel before "The Morenita." The Pope went on to explain that
the love that all Mexicans and Latin Americans in general feel
for the Virgin of Guadalupe is very similar to the devotion that
the Polish people feel for the Black Virgin of Czestochowa. He
was convinced that both were a factor of unity, and were always
at the side of the Mexican and Polish peoples throughout difficult times in their history, even during persecutions they both
endured because they remained true to their faith.

During his first visit to the Basilica of Guadalupe, the Pope
dedicated a beautiful prayer to her, in which he told "The Morenita" that he consecrated to her his entire being and love, his
life, his works, his happiness, as well as his illnesses and suffering. These last words proved to be prophetic, if we consider the
problems and ailments that he had to endure throughout his
pontificate. John Paul II also asked of the Virgin of Guadalupe
for peace, justice, and prosperity for all the peoples of the world.

At the end of the ceremony, the Pope went to the feet of
the Guadalupaña, and visibly moved, he prayed for a long time
before her.

On the eve of his second trip to Mexico in May of 1990,
John Paul II wanted to lead the prayer of the rosary while connected with the Basilica of Guadalupe, through a Vatican Radio
link. On his knees, he asked the Virgin of Guadalupe to

> always guide the steps of the pilgrim Pope through-
> out all the world's paths, and that all ecclesiastic com-
> munities in Mexico ask this for Peter's successor, al-
> ways open to the call to a new evangelization.

While on board the plane that took him back to Mexico he
commented to the news reporters that the Virgin of Guadalupe

plays a maternal role not only for the Mexican people, but also for all members of Latin America's society. Her maternal role is also that of an educator:

> The Virgin of Guadalupe must be a Mother who educates and calls together all the peoples, the Church and all members of Latin American society.

John Paul II's love for the Virgin of Guadalupe became embodied in the beatification and later canonization of Juan Diego. When he beatified him in the Basilica of Guadalupe on May 6, 1990, the Pope stated that the Virgin chose him among the most humble of men for that loving manifestation that is the Guadalupaña apparition.

"Juan Diego," explained John Paul II, "represents all indigenous people because of his simplicity, hope, and trust in God and the Virgin." The Pope, who invoked Juan Diego as the "indigenous people's protector and advocate," affirmed that the recognition of his cult must represent a strong calling to all Mexicans:

> From this privileged place that is Guadalupe, heart of an always faithful Mexico, I wish to convene all the Mexican lay people to commit themselves much more actively in the evangelization of society. You cannot remain indifferent before your brothers' suffering, poverty, corruption, and assaults on the truth and human rights.

In 1992, John Paul II had a chapel dedicated to the Virgin of Guadalupe built in the Vatican Grottoes, in the most privileged site, right next to St. Peter's tomb. When he inaugurated it on May 12, 1990, he affirmed the Marian sanctuary with all the depth of its symbolism, as the spiritual center and unifying factor of Mexico's people and history, "pilgrim all the way to Rome to plant its roots next to the site of St. Peter, foundation of the universal Church's unity."

Another example of John Paul II's love for "The Morenita" was his decision in January of 1999 to proclaim the conclusions of the Synod for America in the Basilica, twenty years after his first visit to Mexico. On the plane, John Paul II, responding to a question from a journalist if it was fair to say that he had a predilection for "The Morenita," said:

> I have the "Virgin Morenita," Our Lady of Guadalupe, in my house. It is interesting that the Americas, from North, Central and South, have decided that the Synod must be concluded in a unique place, which is Guadalupe. All of them decided this. What does that mean? That to all of them, the Virgin of Guadalupe, la Morenita, is and will always truly be the only one.

He continued: "I can't say that I do not have a predilection for the Mexican people. It is a people" – he said jokingly – "that does not let anyone sleep," a clear allusion to the expressions of joy and enthusiasm that accompanied him, day and night, during all of his trips to Mexico.

With the significant gesture of declaring on that occasion the celebration of the Virgin of Guadalupe, "with the liturgical rank of Feast" for all of America, the Pope wanted to "entrust and offer the continent's future to Holy Mary, Mother of Christ and of the Church." By addressing the Virgin of Guadalupe as "evangelizer and Mother of America," recognizing the key role she had in the first evangelization, John Paul II demonstrated the firm hope in his heart that she would also help guide the new evangelization, and promote the flourishing of the Christian way of life.

During that fourth visit to Mexico, John Paul II expressed a dream he had of entering the Virgin's "chamber." The Nuncio, Justo Mullo, made a proposal to him and he accepted immediately. To that end, and before his arrival, a special elevator was built behind the Basilica of Guadalupe's central altar so that the Pope could ascend to the chamber where the image is located, to pray there privately.

With him entered his photographer, Arturo Mari, who after so many years continues to remember the great emotion he shared with the Pope in those moments. When the Pope emerged from the chamber, he thanked Monsignor Mullor and told him how extraordinary it was that the Mexican people could venerate such a significant relic. He added that the tilma, a blanket of Indian origin, should have deteriorated rapidly a few years after having been made, that it was impossible to explain how it remained so well preserved, and that the image of the Virgin of Guadalupe was a constant miracle.

To Cardinal Rivera Carrera, Archbishop of Mexico City, he said: *Com'é bella la Morenita* ("How beautiful the Morenita is").

To see the Pope so impressed, the Cardinal recalled that on one occasion during one of his visits to Rome, and while staying in the Apostolic Palace, the Pope took him to his bedroom to show him that he had the image of the Virgin of Guadalupe on his table. This was the image that, according to tradition, Juan Diego carried with him, and that the Pope had received from a family from San Luis Potosi during his first visit to Mexico.

## Fatima

While covering John Paul II's pontificate, we found the maternal presence of the Virgin of Fatima evident everywhere. This filial love story began on May 13, 1981. John Paul had been Pope for a little more than two years. That day he was the victim of an assassination attempt perpetrated by Ali Agca, a Turkish national, in St. Peter's Square, which could have cost him his life.

"At the moment the bullet hit me, I did not realize that it was the anniversary of when the Virgin appeared to three children in Fatima," John Paul II revealed shortly thereafter. He added that it was his personal secretary who brought it to his attention after the surgical procedure to extract the projectile from his intestine had ended.

During his convalescence, the Pope requested a report about the Fatima apparitions. He studied it meticulously until he reached the conclusion that he owed his life to the Virgin's loving intercession.

One year after the assassination attempt, on May 13, 1982, John Paul II traveled to the Sanctuary of Fatima for the first time to "thank the Virgin for her intercession to save his life and restore his health."

In December of 1983, the Pope visited the man who attempted to assassinate him. Even the same Ali Agca spoke about Fatima: "Why didn't you die?" – he asked the Pope. "I know that I pointed the gun correctly, and that the bullet was devastatingly deadly. Then, why didn't you die? Why is everyone talking about Fatima?"

A year later, John Paul II formalized his devotion and gratitude to the Virgin, by donating the bullet that was extracted from him to the Sanctuary of Fatima. Since 1984, the bullet is in the Sanctuary, lodged in the Marian image's halo.

Likewise, he donated the white fascia that he wore the day of his assassination attempt to the Polish Sanctuary of Jasna Gora, whose Virgin has been venerated by his compatriots as a symbol of national unity for centuries.

In 1991 the Holy Father returned to the Sanctuary of Fatima, where he affirmed that "the Virgin granted me another ten years of life." On more than one occasion he pointed out that he considered all the years of his pontificate following the assassination attempt as a gift by Divine Providence as a result of the Virgin of Fatima's intercession. In his 1982 visit to Fatima, John Paul II solemnly consecrated the entire world to the Immaculate Heart of Mary, following one of the recommendations that the Virgin gave to the three little shepherds.

Two years after an encounter with Sister Lucia, the third and only surviving seer of Fatima, John Paul II repeated the consecration, after writing a letter to the bishops of all five continents for them to join the celebration.

John Paul II returned to Fatima in 2000. The Pope's third visit to the Portuguese sanctuary, to beatify two of the little shepherds, culminated with the anxious revelation that put an end to decades of speculation about the content of the third secret. The Pope had somehow given an indication of it during the beatification homily.

> And once again I would like to celebrate the Lord's goodness to me when I was saved from death after being gravely wounded on May 13, 1981. I also express my gratitude to Bl. Jacinta for the sacrifices and prayers offered for the Holy Father, whom she saw suffering greatly.

Jacinta was one of the shepherds of that region of Portugal who saw the Virgin on May 13, 1917, along her brother Francisco and their cousin Lucia. Francisco and Jacinta died a few years later, victims of the Spanish Flu. What was the Pope referring to when he said that the young seer had seen the "Holy Father suffer so much"?

The answer came shortly thereafter, when at the end of the Mass Cardinal Angelo Sodano, the Vatican's Secretary of State, took the floor to make the announcement that the Pope had commissioned him to deliver.

To begin with, Sodano indicated that the Pope's pilgrimage to Fatima constituted "a gesture of gratitude for the Virgin's protection during this pontificate's years." The Cardinal added that "the protection seemed to also be related to the so-called 'part three' of Fatima's secret," in other words, the only revelation of the Virgin to the little shepherds that had not yet been revealed.

This message, said the Cardinal Secretary of State, "constitutes a prophetic vision comparable to those of the Holy Scriptures."

This means that the details contained within the message's text "do not describe future events with 'photographic details' but rather in a summarized and condensed manner. These events take place on the same stage, in succession, and during an unspecified period of time. It is for this reason that the clue within the message's text can only be symbolic in nature."

It was announced in Fatima that the content of the third secret would be revealed soon. It was hinted that the man who "walks painfully towards the cross among the bodies of the martyred, and falls dead to the ground under firearms' bullets," would be John Paul II, struck by Ali Agca's bullets at St. Peter's Square on May 13, 1981.

## Czestochowa

> The Poles are accustomed to link with this place, this
> shrine, the many happenings of their lives: the vari-
> ous joyful or sad moments, especially the solemn, de-
> cisive moments, the occasions of responsibility, such
> as the choice of the direction for one's life, the choice
> of one's vocation, the birth of one's children, the final
> school examinations, and so many other occasions.
> They are accustomed to come with their problems
> to Jasna Gora to speak of them with their heavenly
> Mother, who not only has her image here, one of the
> best known and most venerated pictures of her in the
> world, but *is specially present here*. She is present in the
> mystery of Christ and of the Church, as the Coun-
> cil teaches. She is present for each and every one of
> those who come on pilgrimage to her, even if only in
> spirit and heart when unable to do so physically.
>
> The Poles are accustomed to do this.

With these words John Paul II explained the significance of
the Marian sanctuary to her people during the Mass celebrated
in the Czestochowa monastery on June 4, 1979 during his first
trip to Poland. Jasna Gora is perfectly framed within the history
of Poland, which chose Mary as their queen and invokes her as
their mother.

> I arrived in Jasna Gora with thousands of other young
> people who wanted to see their Mother. It was a stage
> in my life when I had to decide what vocation to fol-
> low, and looked for answers to my heart's concerns.
> My pilgrimage started in Torun, my Diocese. I walked
> 300 kilometers to reach the sanctuary on the eve of

the Feast of the Assumption. Pilgrims arrived from all over Poland: young and elderly people, entire families, the sick, all of whom prayed, sang and gave testimony along their journey, that neither the numerous and tragic events in their history, nor the long years under the communist regime could snatch from their hearts. It seemed that all roads in Poland led to Czestochowa, like arteries through which blood flows to the heart to become filled with life. Jasna Gora was and continues to be the spiritual center of all Polish people, and the heart upon which faith and hope beat. Here we could be ourselves.

*Monsignor Slawomir Oder*

When John Paul II spoke about Jasna Gora as the place where all Polish people pilgrimaged physically or spiritually seeking answers to questions about their existence, he spoke out of his own personal experience.

The sanctuary of Czestochowa marked Karol Wojtyla's life from his childhood. He visited it with his father. During the Nazi occupation years, he used to visit secretly along with other students. His love of Mary increased more and more during these visits. Being in contact with the intense spirituality of this place, and its significance in the history of Poland, developed his Marian devotion that became reflected on his pontificate's motto: *Totus tuus*. He went on pilgrimage to this sanctuary as priest, bishop, cardinal and Pope.

After having been consecrated as bishop in Wawel's Cathedral on September 28, 1959, the first thing that Karol Wojtyla did was to go to Czestochowa to celebrate his first Mass before the image of the Black Virgin. He entrusted his ministry to her.

To Wojtyla, this sanctuary was a great school of faith, universal love, and patriotism. In it, and like the Polish poet C.K. Norwid said, you could *breathe* God. In his first trip to Poland he revealed that it was there that he learned to be a man of great self-confidence and welcomed Mary into his life. He recalled the words of Cardinal Wyszynski, Primate of Poland, who considered that Jasna Gora had great strength which touched the heart profoundly, and was able to keep the Polish nation united in its faithfulness to God and the Church.

To John Paul II, Czestochowa was a special place for evangelization in which Mary put the cause of freedom before the Polish people, generation after generation.

It gives man liberty as a measure of their dignity, but it also gives it as a task, because man can use liberty for good or evil; for he can either build or destroy with it.

The Pope believed that within the evangelization of Jasna Gora there is a call to live in liberty, and make good use of it to build, and not destroy.

Perhaps the strong emotional charge present in John Paul II's words when he spoke about the monastery of Czestochowa could make us think that he had too close a relationship with his people and the history of his nation.

Nevertheless, and despite this strong bond with the Polish tradition, he never fell into the nationalist trap. He was a father for all. His awareness about his past made him to be more open and attentive to the events of all peoples. Educated as a healthy patriot, he saw in the most precious values in the memory of each people, a beautiful contribution to enrich each other reciprocally. This concept became evident in the way he considered the European integration, of which he was a staunch advocate. The true significance of liberty emerged from the immense spiritual heritage so well guarded in Jasna Gora, which John Paul II presented to the world.

*Monsignor Slawomir Oder*

On the occasion of the Great Jubilee of the Christian Millennium in Poland the Polish episcopate, led by Cardinal Wyszynski, proposed as spiritual preparation, a "novena" that lasted from 1957 to 1965. Its most important element was the pilgrimage of the Virgin's image throughout the country.

It was an extraordinary event that touched people's hearts and even worried the communist regime who feared this event would become an opportunity to manifest social unrest. The pilgrimage was to prepare spiritually and morally for the consecration to Mary, which took place on May 3, 1966, for the liberty of the Church in Poland, and the world.

Young Cardinal Wojtyla elaborated a profound theological commentary in which he underlined the faithful's responsibility towards the Church and the presence of a Christian dimension both in culture and social life.

During the celebration of the millennium the number of faithful who came on pilgrimage to Czestochowa increased impressively. Cardinal Wojtyla gave more than one hundred homilies to different groups of pilgrims.

It was an extraordinary event; if we take into account the communist regime's atheist and secularist pressure at that time. We cannot fail to see how the ideals of liberty and respect for human dignity which emerged with such power and determination in the Solidarity movement, the first independent trade union in Eastern Europe, emerged from this celebration. A very evident sign of the Polish labor movement's Marian matrix was the image of the Black Virgin at Gdansk's shipyard and worn with pride by Lech Walesa on his jacket's lapel. For John Paul II to celebrate in this sanctuary the re-conquest of his nation's sovereignty and liberty was certainly a moving and encouraging experience; it was like experiencing firsthand the manifestation of the Queen of Poland's power. *Monsignor Slawomir Oder*

During his trip to Poland in 1997, three years before the Jubilee celebration of the year 2000, the Pope thanked the Virgin of Czestochowa for the protection of the Church and himself, especially during his 50 years of priesthood and his service on the seat of St. Peter. The Pope entrusted her with the years remaining for the Jubilee, his preparation, as well as that of the entire world as it enters the new millennium with Christ. John Paul II asked the Black Virgin to help the world enter the third millennium of Christianity through the holy door of faith, hope and charity.

The relationship with the Virgin of Czestochowa was constant in John Paul II's life and lasted until the day of his death. It is significant that one of the last things he did on the morning of April 1, 2005, on the eve of his death, was to bless the crowns destined for the Virgin's image at Jasna Gora.

In his letter directed to Jasna Gora's monastic community on that date, the Pope wrote: "I bless these crowns which I offer to the image of the Virgin of Jasna Gora. I join in spirit with the priests who are custodians of the Shrine, and all pilgrims. I entrust the nation, the Church and myself to the Virgin's protection. Totus tuus."                    *Monsignor Slawomir Oder*

## The Cross

Jesus crucified was the true center of his contemplation, even the very heart of his everyday life and all of his decisions.

Everyone who lived at his side realized how in his illness, John Paul II put into practice what he had announced repeatedly when he was healthy, in other words, the priceless value of suffering and affliction in the apostolic Church's commitment in the world.

Since the day of his assassination attempt, during the numerous hospitalizations and surgeries, John Paul II's illnesses were under the gaze of the entire world. He never hid anything, and despite his evident physical and moral suffering, he was able to integrate his increasing physical limitations into his ministries.

After the assassination attempt, the Pope returned several times to the Gemelli Hospital: in July of 1992 because of a tumor in his colon; in 1994 due to the fracture of his right femur; in 1996 due to a dislocated back and acute appendicitis; and finally on February 1, 2005 due to acute laryngotracheitis and laryngeal spasm. Since then his life was a true Via Crucis that concluded with his death two months later, on April 2, 2005.

We were witnesses to how in the early 1990s, the first signs of John Paul II's Parkinson's disease symptoms started to emerge; one of his hands began to tremble, then the other; his step became gradually uncertain; he started to bend forward; he began to drool; his face became rigid, and his lips no longer expanded to smile. The disease robbed him of his physical presence and gestures. We first saw him supporting himself with a cane, with which he even joked with by swinging it like Charlie Chaplin; later seated in all types of thrones, armchairs and mobile support apparatuses; and finally seated permanently in a traditional wheelchair. John Paul II accepted that God, who had given him all his gifts, was now taking them away one by one. The Pope, a sportsman, attractive, smiling, polyglot, full of energy, became an invalid, with a rigid face and his body paralyzed by Parkinson's.

> During the last weeks of his life, and after the tracheotomy procedure he was subjected to because he could no longer breathe on his own, he lost his voice, one of his most fascinating instruments. The Pope, who was the voice of those who did not have one, became silent forever. *Valentina Alazraki*

In all of these situations, John Paul II demonstrated great strength. Few people in the world, few heads of state or governments would have accepted to share so many limitations with such humility. He continued to proclaim the Gospel on a personal Via Crucis that he carried with enormous dignity, a spirit of obedience and acceptance. The man who had tried to teach us how to live also taught us how to die.

John Paul II never seriously thought about resigning – despite the fact that he considered that possibility in the event he could not carry out his mission – because he believed that the moment in which a Christian has more pastoral possibilities is precisely when he finds himself under the cross of illness and misery. This is why we never saw in him a gesture or a hint of his being willing to resign. He accepted his progressive disability as another phase in his service to the Church.

He used to say that Christ had not come down from His cross; therefore he would not do so either.

Dr. Rodolfo Proietti, who supervised his care at the Gemelli Hospital, told us that during all of his admissions to the hospital, he asked to be allowed to communicate with the outside world. The medical staff tried to help him, but it became very complicated during his last two admissions before and after the tracheotomy procedure, as his physical stamina became critical. The Pope however, showed great stubbornness, and did not mind the enormous effort it took for him to look out the window from his hospital room.

The people who came to see him in St. Peter's Square or at Gemelli Hospital could see the will that the Pope both demonstrated and transmitted through the strength and courage of his example.

The physicians who took care of him over the years were also witnesses of his great capacity to tolerate pain and how he attempted to hide his sufferings, especially when Sister Tobiana and his secretary were in his presence, to avoid upsetting them.

In 1994, after surgery to repair the fracture of his right femur, John Paul II hinted at it as his spiritual journey to the cross of Christ.

> I have understood that I must carry the Church of Christ to this third millennium with prayer and diverse initiatives, but I have also seen that this is not

enough; I needed to do so with suffering, with the assassination attempt of thirteen years ago, and now with this new sacrifice. Why now? Why in this the Year of the Family? Precisely because the family is threatened, he too is attacked. The Pope must be attacked, the Pope must suffer for all the families and the world to see that there is – one could say – a superior Gospel: a gospel of suffering, with which we must prepare the future, the third millennium of each and every family.

Two years later, during a serious operation for appendicitis, when referring to his physical suffering he told his spokesman, Joaquin Navarro Valls, that whatever remains of the passion of Christ must be fulfilled in our bodies, in our flesh, because although it is finished, you can always add something more.

During a trip to Sarajevo in April 1997 and despite having suffered from cardiac problems, according to his personal physician he still wanted to celebrate Mass in the snow. John Paul II spent the entire ceremony trembling from both the extremely cold temperatures and the ill effects of Parkinson's. His Master of Ceremonies, Monsignor Marini, squeezed his hand to cheer him on, while his secretary tried to cover him with his red cape. The Pope remained firm until the end. When he returned to the sacristy Monsignor Marini told him how much he regretted that he had to endure such conditions. He even apologized, telling him that perhaps they should have protected the altar better. John Paul II responded that what he suffered on that day was nothing compared with what that city and their people had suffered. In some way he was glad to have had the opportunity to share in their suffering.

During the cause for his beatification, special emphasis was made about the fact that John Paul II's will to associate his suffering with Christ's for the good of humanity and the Church, was decisive proof of his heroism in practicing all the virtues.

Since his youth, John Paul II knew very well what suffering was. At the age of twenty-four, and on his way back from work in a factory in Cracow, he was hit by a German army truck. His apparently lifeless body ended up in a ditch. He woke up in the hospital with his head bandaged. He was told that a woman had found and assisted him, but no one could identify her. The woman disappeared. That was the first time that he was certain about having been saved by the Virgin Mary.

As a child and as a youth he endured the pain of the soul due to the death of all his loved ones. Karol Wojtyla lost his mother when he was only nine years old. One day, when he returned home from school he found her dead. The pain from that sudden loss became embodied years later in the poem titled *A Voice singing in another room, before all was silent*. Four years later his brother Edmund passed away, a young doctor who was infected by a patient suffering from scarlet fever. His friends recalled that when a teacher offered him his condolences on his brother's death, young Karol, showing great maturity, responded: "I accept God's will."

Karol and his father were alone.

Years later, after the outbreak of the Second World War and Germany's invasion of Poland, upon returning from the quarry where he worked, he once again stumbled upon death in his own home. His father had passed away. Karol, who was twenty-one years old, was now completely alone in the world.

He remained in vigil over his father all night on his knees and praying. His friends believe that within that strong pain and desolation, he heard God's voice calling out to him.

One of the most moving images of his last year of life was that of the Pope kneeling in the Grotto of the Apparitions at Lourdes. John Paul II chose that sanctuary of suffering for his last voyage, number one hundred and four of his itinerant pontificate. He was on the verge of falling during his visit because his knees could no longer support the weight of his body. He then told the world that he felt that he had reached the finish line of his pilgrimage.

Like another sick man on his knees in the Grotto of the Virgin's apparitions to Bernadette, he was moved and sobbed, took water from the fountain of miracles and spent the night at the Notre Dame residence, a center for sick and disabled pilgrims.

The image of John Paul II clutching at the kneeler, with his face resting on it while dangerously slipping to the point of almost falling, is unforgettable. The next day he could not even pronounce his message and prayer to the Virgin, in which he begs her to teach him to remain close to her and near "the numerous crosses throughout the world."

During the Mass of the Feast of the Assumption, the Pope had to interrupt the reading of his homily three times. We attendees realized the gravity of his condition and respiratory problems, which were evident and would become more acute later on. We could hear through the open microphone when he asked his secretary for assistance in Polish. Don Estanislao (Fr. Stanislaw Dziwisz) handed him a glass of water. Talking to himself he said: *Musze siconczyc,* which means "I must finish." He was able to do so supported by the applause of the sick, who tried to encourage him.

What was most impacting in these thrilling days was that the sick who arrived at Lourdes were of less ill health than the

Pope. However, they drew strength from him. It was something absolutely paradoxical. However, these sick people saw in him an example to follow in bearing and accepting suffering. They understood that he reached the end of his earthly existence totally committed to the Father, accepting his suffering, and finally death, with serenity.

At the conclusion of this trip that saddened and worried the entire world, one of the cardinals who had accompanied him acknowledged that John Paul II was aware that death was near.

Dr. Renato Buzzonetti, his personal physician was struck by the testimony John Paul II gave at Lourdes:

> At no time did he hide his impotence as a sick man; without conventional modesties, and with the simplicity of the just man, he declared his faithfulness to life, a gift from God, without escapes or shortcuts. A great catechesis had been taught, one that celebrated sickness in lieu of the crucifix, not as humiliation or condemnation, but as a gift of grace and sublime song to human life.

Throughout his entire life, John Paul II showed a great deal of attention to the sick. He encountered them in every one of his audiences and travels, and dedicated a lot of time to them. He spoke to them about the meaning of pain, the dignity of suffering, and a way in which it could be offered for the well-being of the world and the Church.

It is not a coincidence that the first time he stepped outside the Vatican the next day after his election he went to Gemelli Hospital to visit a great Polish friend of his, Monsignor Deskur, who suffered from an extremely serious illness. That same day he affirmed that he wanted to dedicate his pontificate to those who suffer.

The Pope not only visited his friend; he also entered the section of the hospital reserved for the terminally ill to caress them, speak to them, and try to comfort them. On that day nobody could have imagined that the Gemelli Hospital would become his third home. John Paul II got to calling it "Vatican Number Three" because of the impressive number of days he spent during his seven admissions there.

The longest and most dramatic was the first, in the wake of the attack that nearly cost him his life. John Paul II arrived at the hospital after having lost a great amount of blood in the ambulance that transported him to the emergency room and which on that day had its siren out of order. Lying on the back of the ambulance, with his secretary supporting his head, he did nothing but repeat with an almost inaudible voice: "Jesus, Mary, my mother." The people who remained at his side on May 13, 1981 were impressed by his strength. His personal assistant, Angelo Gugel, who was in the jeep next to the driver, narrated that after the Pope was wounded, he rushed to the back of the ambulance and supported his head. He put his arm around his neck and saw how much he had bled. John Paul II did not complain. He was serene, and to the chief of police in charge of security at St. Peter's Square he said repeatedly in a very low tone of voice, "Thanks, inspector."

In the midst of enormous confusion and agitation, the Pope was first taken to the room on the tenth floor that had been prepared for him since the beginning of his pontificate and, upon realizing the error, the medical team promptly transferred him to the operating room where Fr. Stanislaw imparted absolution and Extreme Unction. The Pope was on the threshold of death.

The surgical intervention lasted more than five hours. Upon exiting the operating room he was taken to the Intensive Care Unit. He woke up from the anesthesia the next day. On May 17, through Vatican Radio, we could hear his weak voice. From his bed, without any strength, he said: "Priest and victim, I offer my sufferings for the world and the Church." He also forgave the person who had attempted to take his life.

The Pope's pain in those days was not only physical. Four days after the assault, Italy approved the law which legalized abortion within the first three months of pregnancy. Within days, Cardinal Wyszynski, primate of Poland, passed away. Before the conclave of 1978 he predicted that he, John Paul II, would be tasked with carrying humanity towards the third millennium.

A Polish friend, Professor Stanislaw Grygiel, observed that "God had used him in cruel fashion." John Paul II responded that there is nothing better for a priest than to be used by God.

It is also not a coincidence that in the first message he pronounced in the Sistine Chapel on the day after his election, John Paul II addressed the sick to tell them that he needed their help, their prayers, and their sacrifice. The sick understood that he, especially in the latter years of his life, was another sick man, and that no one better than he could understand them; express his affection and proximity to them. On some occasions his collaborators had to inform him that he had to cut his encounters short because their program was delayed, but the Pope responded that one could not be in a hurry with those who suffer.

We witnessed his warmth towards the sick on many occasions, whether they were infected with the AIDS virus, leprosy, cancer, or were disabled. He was very affectionate with them, and did not fear their contact. He showed both a spiritual and concrete love for the weak.

The Pope's photographer, Arturo Mari, told us about having witnessed the time when he caressed and embraced the sick at a leprosarium in the Busan Strait, South Korea. At that moment, Mari tried to imagine what these lepers felt when the Pope was returning their dignity to them as human beings.

There are two moments that will forever remain among the images about the Pope's approach to pain and suffering: His visit to Kalighat, the Home of the Pure Heart of Calcutta established in Calcutta, India, by Mother Teresa, where he blessed the dying, and his first encounter in the Mission Dolores Basilica in San Francisco, California.

## With those Sick from AIDS and the Sick of Mother Teresa

John Paul II entered the Home of the Pure Heart with Mother Teresa. The first thing he saw was a blackboard with that day's date, February 4, 1985, followed by several pieces of information: "Number of sick people admitted: 2; Released: 0; Deceased: 4." The Pope toured the two large dormitories, one for men and the other for women; he approached each one of the dying and traced the sign of the cross on their foreheads. Mother Teresa, always with a smile on her lips, began to serve dinner, assisted by the Sisters of Charity. The Pope did the same. Later on he wanted to enter the small mortuary, where the four people who had died earlier that day had been placed: two men; one child and one woman. Only the child carried a small cross on his chest, he was Catholic. Right when the Pope was about to exit the house, a sobbing woman's screams could be heard. The Pope approached her. Mother Teresa translated from Bengali: "I find myself terribly alone" – said the woman shedding tears and added – "Father please come back to see us."

The Pope was deeply moved. Upon exiting the Home of the Pure Heart he spoke about the "city of happiness." About human suffering, and death he said: "This place is 'a testimony to the primacy of love and charity,' where the 'mystery of human suffering meets the mystery of faith and love.'"

Years later, his enormous charity towards the sick took him to Mission Dolores Basilica in San Francisco, California, to become close to the AIDS drama for the first time. The Pope was received by sixty or so patients, accompanied by their relatives, partners, and nurses.

John Paul II greeted, embraced and blessed each one of them to demonstrate his compassion, and not his condemnation for the victims of what some prelates qualified during those years as "the scourge of God," the result of behaviors contrary to sexual morals. Fred Powell, fifty-two years old and Catholic, was among them, and after the Pope left he commented: "The fact that John Paul II has come to us to embrace and bless us, is the beginning of a new light that will go around the world, and illuminate a lot of people."

At the Basilica, the Pope said that "God loves everyone without distinction; those who are suffering from AIDS; their relatives and friends who care for them." His words and gestures not only reflected his own charity, but also represented an invitation to all of those who still had many prejudices, to charity as well.

The most moving moment of the encounter came when John Paul II kissed a five-year-old child, infected with AIDS due to a blood transfusion, who was accompanied by his parents. It was also very impressive to see the Pope next to a priest who had also contracted the disease. At the end of the encounter several patients expressed that, through the Pope's charity, they had understood that God's love reaches out to everyone equally.

The nurses who cared for him day and night until the end of his life were witnesses to how John Paul II accepted his increasing physical impotence, his respiratory difficulties due to Parkinson's, and his inability to move – with complete abandonment to the will of God.

The medical assistance he received was guaranteed by specialists and nurses. At the end he could not speak, but still expressed his gratitude by a blessing gesture with his hand. He was obedient, and did what the doctors and nurses asked of him. The difficulties he experienced when trying to swallow and feed himself, as well as the repeated cleanings of the catheter caused him enormous suffering, but he still demonstrated great patience. During the last days he spent at the hospital, he repeated frequently that St. Peter had been crucified upside down.

> Very near the end, when he was barely able to speak, we witnessed his impotent struggle: we saw how he struck the lectern once he realized he could not speak, but we also witnessed that even three days before his death he renounced going to his bedroom window to bless the faithful who were bidding him farewell. He would put his hand on the cannula (breathing tube) that was put in place after his tracheotomy, to make us understand that he would have liked to continue to communicate with the world, but that it was no longer possible, at least not with words. However, his strength, his last form of communication, although he was totally silent, continued to speak to us with even greater vigor.

An inerasable image was that of John Paul II with

his back turned to us in his private chapel during his last Good Friday. He did not want to show his face because he was carrying the cannula from his trache-otomy. Many people are still marked by the figure of the sick Pope, bent forward, with his hands clasped and saliva dripping over them, unable to speak in a comprehensible fashion, with a gaze that expressed the suffering from his illness. Every time they saw him they were reminded of Christ on the cross.

*Valentina Alazraki*

Doctor Renato Buzzonetti evoked John Paul II's death with poignant words upon realizing that:

The electrocardiogram registered the end of a great earthly adventure for a man already invoked as a saint by the people of God. John Paul II's death was that of a man stripped of almost everything, who had lived hours of battle and of glory and who now presented himself in his nakedness to meet his Lord.

John Paul II's personal physician was present on Saturday April 2, 2005 at 3:30 P.M. when the Pope told Mother Tobiana with an almost imperceptible voice: "Let me go to the house of the Father." Doctor Buzzonetti stated:

His was not a passive surrender to the disease, or an escape from suffering, but the expression of a pro-found consciousness of a Via Crucis that neared the finish line: they were words of hope, of a renewed and definitive abandonment in the hands of the Father.

## Mercy

One of the fundamental elements of John Paul II's spirituality was his devotion to the Divine Mercy. Throughout his entire life, he knew that this is the true hope for man. People alone cannot construct their future and assure their happiness: their only hope is the heart of Christ that communicates God's mercy and compassion towards man: it is a call to communion with Him.

The Pope wrote the encyclical *Dives in misericordia* through which he actively promoted the cult of Divine Mercy. As Cardinal and Archbishop of Cracow, Karol Wojtyla promoted the cause of the beatification of Mother Faustina Kowalska, the apostle of Divine Mercy. As Pope he beatified her on April 18, 1993, the day of the Feast of the Divine Mercy; he canonized her seven years later, on April 30, 2000, the Sunday of the Divine Mercy. (Divine Mercy Sunday is the Sunday after Easter; it can fall on a variety of dates.) St. Faustina possesses the honor of being the first saint canonized in the third millennium.

Additionally, during his trip to Poland in 2002, John Paul II trusted the world to the Divine Mercy. His devotion to the Divine Mercy – which marked him profoundly – and his death are intimately related: John Paul passed away on Saturday April 2, the day before the Sunday that year on which the Feast of the Divine Mercy, which he instituted in 2000, was celebrated. The last Mass that John Paul II attended was at 8:00 P.M. and dedicated to the Divine Mercy.

The next day, during the Mass after his death which Cardinal Angelo Sodano (the Vatican's Secretary of State whom all of us called "the voice of the Pope" because it was he who would "lend" his voice to the Pope after the tracheotomy intervention that left him unable to speak) celebrated, he read the *Angelus* that John Paul II had prepared for that Sunday.

In it, the Pope made special emphasis on the need of the world to understand and embrace the Divine Mercy: "Lord, who with your death and resurrection reveal the Father's love, we believe in you and with trust we repeat: 'Lord Jesus, today I put my trust in you, have mercy on us and on the entire world.'"

His beatification, which took place on May 1, 2011, was also celebrated on Divine Mercy Sunday. April 27, 2014, the day on which the Divine Mercy was celebrated in 2014, was chosen for his canonization as well.

As a youth, and in the years he worked as a laborer at the Solvay factory during the Nazi occupation, Karol Wojtyla visited the chapel of the Order to which Sister Faustina belonged on a daily basis. He recalled this when he traveled to Poland for the last time to consecrate the new Divine Mercy Sanctuary in 2002.

The last century turned over to history two totalitarianisms that left human suffering, extermination camps, the Gulag, hatred, poverty, and hunger as a legacy. Communism and Nazism put man through despair, turmoil, and darkness.

John Paul II, who had to confront the evils of both totalitarianisms during the past century, with their terrible and devastating consequences, wanted to give a consoling, inspiring and hopeful testimony to the Church and the world. This is both the testimony and mystical experience of St. Faustina Kowalska.

The message from this simple, religious woman, who received the gift of mystical visions, expresses a strong conviction of forgiveness, of the possibility to become a new creation, through a complete change

and transformation sustained by Divine Grace, and
tasked with a renewed spirit and heart.

*Monsignor Slawomir Oder*

During the general audience of October 24, 2001, John
Paul II stated:

> "Even if our sins were as black as the night, Divine
> Mercy is greater than our misery. Only one thing is
> needed: the sinner has to leave the door to his heart
> ajar... God can do the rest.... Everything begins and
> ends with his mercy," so writes St. Faustina Kowalska.

To the Pope, the profound understanding of this truth constituted the heart of the Christian message, the source of Christian optimism, and the foundation of man's true liberty.

Great enthusiasm and a profound hope were transparent in
John Paul's actions, words and attitudes, which emerged from a
great understanding of the Divine Mercy, and they assumed a
very precise form; on one hand, he abandoned himself to God's
mercy, while at the same time he had a strong sense of responsibility to be at the service of his brothers and sisters as minister
of this mercy.

It was about practicing an active mercy open to the love of
God and one's fellow man.

John Paul II maintained that the mercy received does not
take away man's dignity; quite the contrary, since based upon
the experience of the goodness received, it directs man towards
his own truth, his origins and true vocation. Mercy is placed in
a lost and sinning man's path, as a gift of hope and liberation, as
a gift of a new creation.

Indeed, God saves men, not thanks to their good deeds and actions, but thanks to His infinite mercy. John Paul II was convinced that the sacrament of reconciliation is the sacrament that opens man's heart wide open to embrace the gift of mercy, and transforms it in witness of God's free gift.

It is the Divine Mercy which propels mankind on a path of justice and active charity.

The Polish Pope used to say that "mercy is invoked in every continent from the most profound human suffering. For peace to emerge, the grace of mercy is needed to placate hearts and minds wherever there is thirst for hatred and revenge, where war results in the suffering and death of innocents. God's merciful love is needed wherever respect for life and man's dignity have disappeared, for it is under its light that each human being's inexplicable worth is demonstrated."

In his homily of August 17, 2002, during the consecration of the Divine Mercy Sanctuary in Lagiewniki, Cracow, John Paul II concluded with a prayer that I would like to recall:

God, Merciful Father,
who have revealed Your love in Your Son Jesus Christ,
and have poured Him over us via the consoling Holy Spirit:
We trust the destiny of the world and each man's to You.
Lean on us sinners,
strengthen our weakness,
defeat all evil.
Make all inhabitants of the Earth experience your mercy,
so that in You, One and Triune God,
they always find a source of hope.
Eternal Father,
by Your Son's painful passion and resurrection,
have mercy on us and on the entire world.
Amen.                                    *Monsignor Slawomir Oder*

# 3  John Paul II's Humanity

Christianity is the religion of the Incarnation. John Paul II was Pope, but he was also a man. He knew how to live an authentic life. As a man he achieved the ideal of a Christian life, demonstrating to us that sanctity is not separated from daily life. His sanctity was the result of an extraordinarily rich and profound humanity, lived with transparency, sparing no effort or energy.

Without a doubt, his secret was to show God's human face. The people who followed him were not so much looking for him as they were looking for God's person, of whom he was witness. Joaquin Navarro Valls, the man who was his spokesman for more than twenty years, affirmed that on one occasion John Paul II personified this truth, expressing it with clear gestures, in comprehensible manifestations, through indelible images that not only revealed Wojtyla the man, but also revealed the content of the faith and its application in specific moments in life. Long before becoming Pope, he already possessed that innate capacity to reveal the faith through visible signs.

Among the documents collected and analyzed by the historical commission during the beatification process, several reports from the Communist Secret Service about Karol Wojtyla came to light, from his time as a seminarian to his years as Cardinal and Archbishop of Cracow.

In them he is described as a very dangerous person because morally he possessed extraordinary human and spiritual qualities, without any suspicious or ambiguous relationships, and no interest in material things. They spoke about him as a true leader, with great intelligence who does not impose, but rather knows how to organize people in order to achieve common goals; who knows how to attract the simple people, the youth and intellectuals as well. He is pictured as a man of dialogue, but inflexible at the same time, who accepts compromise, but not about irrefutable truths.

His humble attitude gave the impression that his actions were not extraordinary. However, people perceived that in reality he was a man out of the ordinary. There was a sense of being before a person truly sent by God to be among men. The reactions that he elicited were not ordinary: before him people kneeled, prayed, cried, sang, and were moved. Even in non-Catholic countries, or at least cold from a religious practice point of view, the same emotions were observed.

One of the men in charge of John Paul II's security from the beginning of his pontificate summarized the evolution of people's sentiment in one phrase: "At the beginning, when the Pope came near the barricades to greet the people, he heard the women say: 'How handsome he is!' As the years went by, what was mostly heard was: 'What a saint he is!'"

John Paul II was a very simple man who did not like special attentions, neither inside nor outside the Vatican. He behaved like any other person; he even adapted better than other people to uncomfortable situations. He never gave any importance to comforts or amenities.

When he visited an African, Latin American or Asian country he never complained about weather conditions or the precarious lodging conditions to which he needed to adapt. These trips affected his nightly rest, but he never asked for anything to help him sleep. Upon returning from a distant country he would spend several days adjusting to the time zone change, without complaining. His collaborators realized that his sleep was altered because sometimes, and for several days after having returned from a trip, he would ask them if they could sleep at night.

When he left the Vatican secretly to go to the mountains, he always asked for a car that attracted little attention. In these excursions he enjoyed eating bread with ham, or a piece of homemade cheese while sitting on the grass next to his secretary and those in charge of his security. He was a man without any pretensions whatsoever. With the exception of the chapels to pray, and the pool in which to exercise, he did not request any remodeling of the apartments where he lived, whether it was in Poland, the Vatican, at Castelgandolfo or in the mountains. In his Vatican apartment he kept Paul VI's furniture, including his old television. His room was very simple. He never paid attention to the furniture, paintings or rugs around him.

He was not interested in luxury because he was always a man without any attachment to material possessions. He was born into a middle class family, was educated in an atmosphere of sacrifice and self-denial, and always lived a life without luxuries or comforts. Since he was a child he became accustomed to renounce the superfluous.

During his fourth visit to Mexico a painting of Botticelli was placed in the nunciature's chapel. Upon exiting the chapel, Nuncio Justo Mellor asked the Pope if he liked the painting. The Pope, who had not even noticed it, responded that he had entered the chapel to admire the tabernacle, and that no art piece from any museum in the world had much value to him.

Those who knew him in his years as a seminarian have pointed out that he wore a much worn cassock, shoes that were in very bad shape, and a backpack that was in even worse condition. Those who knew him when he was a priest, and later Auxiliary Bishop of Cracow, remember that he traveled by train in second class, and that his automobiles were dilapidated.

Just as in his youth, he also resisted wearing new clothes during his papacy. He asked that his tunics be mended, and skied with old-fashioned attire that no one wore anymore. While in Cracow he had very few shirts, and during one very hot summer, he cut their sleeves. When winter arrived, he had nothing to wear. People wanted to buy new clothes for him, but knowing that he would not accept them, they would buy clothes and then soil and wash them several times to make them look worn.

After a visit to the United States, Polish immigrants gave him a new car, a Ford. During a pastoral visit he heard a child say: "Look, what a nice car!" He stopped using the car because he did not want the faithful to remember him because of the car he drove but because of his ministry.

When he was Cardinal he would arrive at the Vatican with much worn hiking boots and a very old briefcase. When he arrived at the offices of the people with whom he had appointments, including his friend Monsignor Deskur, he never accepted to enter ahead of the others who were already waiting. He waited his turn as if he were the last of the pastors.

His relationship with material possessions did not change during his pontificate. He had no more than two cassocks, and demanded that they be mended. The nuns who assisted him in the mountain residence, Lorenzago di Cadore, where he spent several summer vacations, narrated that on one occasion he arrived with underwear so worn that it irritated his skin. They bought new underwear for him, and John Paul II complained sweetly about the initiative they had taken on his behalf.

He could not stand new shoes. He wore the old ones as much as possible to become used to them and feel more comfortable. Neither did he like the papal clothing for official ceremonies. For many years those responsible for the protocol "made" him dress in accordance with the circumstances, with cowl and surplice, until at the end of his pontificate he won the battle and even received heads of state in his white cassock.

Cardinal Joachim Meisner, Archbishop of Cologne, commented on one occasion that John Paul II gave the impression that all of his wealth was God Himself, and that he gave no importance to things of this world. "It was always my impression that the Pope lived poorly inside a golden cage," he added.

John Paul II was attracted by human contact; this was very important to him, and why he loved sharing meals with priests, bishops or cardinals passing through Rome, or with his collaborators. He never ate alone.

According to his Polish friends, first Karol Wojtyla, then John Paul II, gave himself to others in an extraordinary fashion. On one occasion his friend Grygiel went to dinner at his house, accompanied by his son who was eight years old at the time. The child was bored and would kick him below the table. The Pope realized the situation and asked him what was wrong, to which the child responded with sincerity. John Paul told him: "You are right; I invited you to my home and have not taken care of you. I apologize." From that moment on he played and joked with him.

John Paul II ate very moderately. He did not ask for special meals, and ate what he was given without ever complaining.

Neither did he show any particular taste for food; he was sober in his nutrition and did not like refined dishes. His favorite dish was an egg omelet. He loved candy, but renounced it frequently. He would not prevent his table companions from consuming alcoholic beverages, but he at the most, would join to make a toast. When he was offered something to eat, he would barely taste it, only to be thankful.

The process of his beatification put in evidence that despite having continuous commitments and the need to face numerous problems, many times very disturbing and serious ones, John Paul II always showed a great deal of self-control and serenity.

He worked very hard, but managed his time very well in order to tend to work, prayer and audiences. However, he also knew how to rest as well, for example by going on excursions both in Poland and Italy. According to his collaborators, John Paul II did not manifest noticeable mood changes; his emotional equilibrium and inner peace were evident. In fact, his sense of humor never abandoned him, neither during difficult moments nor unexpected ones.

His extraordinary inner freedom attracted a lot of attention; to know how to live without stress, and not allow any kind of pressure to defeat him; to be free to show affection; to know how to build relationships with a variety of people, and the simplest people; to know how to make the most advantage of his time. During long plane trips, the entire papal entourage, journalists included, tried to rest, while he read, prayed the breviary or wrote the text for the general audience to which he dedicated the balance of his visit. Anytime there was a delay, he would take advantage of it by reading or praying.

Although he looked like an extrovert, he did not enjoy speaking that much; he preferred to work and pray. His rest consisted of reading a book; he always carried several with him.

He did not take care of his health excessively, and his collaborators had to remind him that he had to keep his efforts in check. Even when he was very ill, he always resisted shortening his commitments or trips. He believed that as long as God granted him life, he had to do everything he could without sparing any effort.

## Man of Love

> "Love is not something you learn,
> even though there is nothing
> that is more necessary to learn."
> John Paul II, *Crossing the Threshold of Hope*

John Paul II was convinced that he was loved. To him, the awareness of God's great love, and the worth of every human being in His eyes, was the basic foundation of a true Christian life.

John Paul II sowed much love and, through his example, gave people the certainty that they were loved. He incarnated universal paternity in an extraordinary fashion, even with people from other religions and non-believers. The most visible sign of this love was his desire to spread God's message throughout the entire world, to search the heart of man and convince it to love God.

His mission was received like that of a father. At twenty years old, Karol Wojtyla no longer had any one from his family, but from that moment, gradually, first through his mission in Poland, and then in the Vatican, he made the world family his own. When he passed away, to the great majority of the faithful who had followed him for more than twenty-six years and felt accompanied by him, a member of the family had died. In the several thousands of letters that were left at his grave or sent to the Postulator's Office since his death, he is called "papa," "Lolek," "Karol," "Uncle," "grandfather," "father."

What transpired at his funeral, when more than three million people arrived in Rome to bid him farewell, is evident proof. He was the head of the Catholic Church, but the openness of his heart, his mind, his arms, towards the non-believing people, or those who even may have believed in another god, made them all feel that they were appreciated and taken into account.

From very early in his youth, he distinguished himself from his friends by the way in which he demonstrated his love for others.

Jerzy Kluger, John Paul II's Jewish friend with whom he maintained a bond from his childhood through the end of his life, told how on one occasion, after finishing elementary school and because he lived closer to the school than Karol, he went over to see the test results. Upon not finding him at his house, Jerzy went to the church where his friend was serving as altar boy. When he saw him, Karol signaled to him not to speak. A very sanctimonious woman recognized him and very angrily asked him if he was the son of Doctor Kluger, whom everyone knew was Jewish. He, following Karol's instructions, did not speak. At the end of the Mass, upon knowing what had happened, the future Pope told his friend: "Does that lady not know that we are all God's children?"

On another occasion, while in prep school, a school janitor who used to get drunk was struck by a car. All the students went to the street but did not take any initiative. Karol went looking for a priest to provide him with spiritual assistance. To do this would not have occurred to any other boy.

Throughout his life, John Paul II treated his friends, whether they were simple or very important people, his students and professors, in the same manner, with great warmth and friendship. He never kept his distance. He listened to their problems and tribulations and provided counsel. His particular sensitivity made people feel loved in a unique way. A gaze from him was sufficient to feel his love. When the Pope directed his gaze towards a crowd, everyone got the impression that he was looking specifically at them. They all felt included, the targets of his special attention.

His love for the poor, the weak and the children stood out throughout his life. He was always very generous with them and since his youth he would give his clothes and everything he had to them. On one occasion when he was a young priest, he had to celebrate Mass at St. Florian Parish but could not get there. When people went looking for him they realized that he had no shoes. He had given them to another student the night before, as well as a sweater that the nuns had knitted for him.

On several trips we witnessed the Pope carry out symbolic acts, because he believed in them as part of the diffusion of the Gospel. For example, during a visit to a favela in Rio de Janeiro, Brazil in 1980, he decided to enter a shack where a very elderly woman lived. He blessed her, kissed her on the cheeks and at the end took off his ring and gave it to her.

John Paul II also demonstrated his love for prison inmates, whom he visited on several occasions both in Italy and during his trips. The Pope's visit to Durango's Rehabilitation Center during his second trip to Mexico in 1990 remains an inerasable one. Contrary to what security agents had requested of him, he wanted to mingle with the prisoners: he crossed the threshold of their cells to greet them one by one; he caressed and embraced them. Many of them wept. The Pope told them that the worst of prisons was a closed and hardened heart, but the worst of evils was despair. He assured them that he would pray for them and ask God to give them "hope to occupy a normal place in society, to find a new and dignified life."

It was amazing that, to mark the first anniversary of John Paul II's death, General Wojciech Jaruzelski, who was a witness to the cause of his beatification, said that on several occasions he had felt the Pope's sanctity, and that it was that sanctity which modified his own attitude both at a personal and political level. One of the examples he cited was precisely the Pope's visit to the Durango prison. "It was during that encounter, where the Pope paid no attention to the security guards, that we witnessed his enormous moral dimension. If anyone wants to qualify it as sanctity, then they are in their right to do so."

There was a great deal of respect for the human being in his way of showing love. The Pope disliked anyone to speak ill against another, much less to spread rumors and gossip against anyone. His closest collaborators on many occasions commented that they never heard him speak ill about anyone. Rarely did he give a negative opinion about anyone; most of the time he simply remained quiet.

He prayed for the conversion of his enemies. He always searched for clarification, or a solution to conflicts and misunderstanding. When he was a young bishop he promoted the drafting of a letter that the Polish bishops sent to the German bishops as a sign of reconciliation after the Nazi occupation of Poland. He was also one of the first bishops to visit the Church in East Germany.

As pontiff, he continued to be humble with his collaborators. A Swiss guard who guarded the hallway of the papal apartment one Christmas night, when the Cardinals of the curia stop by to congratulate the Pope, was impressed by the fact that the only person who congratulated him was John Paul II. He actually came out of his apartment to do it. He was constantly making others feel that they were more important that he was. He always felt it a privilege to make a direct and personal contact with others, to speak with and greet them. In every encounter, he always took the time to give himself to others.

One of John Paul II's greatest manifestations of love towards God and man was his travels. On many occasions he explained that he did not want to live in a palace, isolated like a monarch, because his place was among people, and he could not ignore the humanity that surrounded him. Travel was a moral imperative to him. As pastor of the universal Church he felt compelled to take the word of God to the most remote corners of the world to demonstrate with his presence that God loves everyone without distinction of race, culture, and even religion.

He was a tireless traveler during twenty-six years; not even during his last year of life did he renounce doing it. He presented himself before the world as a pilgrim, a prophet, sometimes a crusader, inspired by a visible and missionary urgency that emerged from the conviction that only a world that recognizes God can be worthy of man.

From his first travels he understood that the message had to be joined by a presence, because making oneself present anywhere in the planet represented a signal of solidarity, of participation in the history of a people or nation. To those who criticized his large number of trips he responded that if he did not do it, he would be labeled as being indifferent to what happens in the world.

Because of love, the Pope traveled three times the distance

between the Earth and the Moon, with his only objective being to give continuous and public testimony to the faith. With him, faith emerged from both its physical and moral catacombs. One of his achievements was that the faithful were once again proud to be Catholics, and stopped being afraid to manifest that pride. This was seen in Mexico, Poland, the Eastern European countries and Cuba among many others.

As the third millennium approached, he invited all believers to follow him, to continue with that missionary spirit and love. His calling was clear: "Let's hoist our sails and navigate in the open sea to announce the Gospel everywhere."

## Love of Man

Authentic love for God is inseparable from the love for our fellow man. A man who loved God as intensely as John Paul II did could not avoid being an exemplary testimony of dedication to others.

Monsignor Vincenzo Paglia, general ecclesiastical adviser for the Community of St. Egidio and president of the Pontifical Council for the Family created by John Paul II, on many occasions was witness to the passion that John Paul II had for people. Shortly after the assault, and during a dinner that he shared with the Pope, they watched a television program that debated whether or not the Pope should continue to approach the crowds during his general audiences. The Pope only commented: "The shepherd is always with his sheep; it is a life condition that acquires even more importance when the sheep are in danger."

John Paul II made his pontificate a crusade in favor of man. He was convinced that the human being is "the first path that the Church must traverse to carry out its mission." The word that the Pope pronounced the most was "man," and it is no coincidence that he dedicated his first encyclical, *Redemptor hominis*, precisely to the human being. He explained that a Pope born in a diocese whose territory includes the Auschwitz concentration camp, could not avoid dedicating his first papal document to the cause of humanity, to the threats against men and their inalienable rights.

His conviction that man had been created in God's image and likeness, made John Paul II's defense of the primacy of the human being to mean primarily the defense of the sacred right to life. The person's inviolability from the moment of conception until natural death was to John Paul II the starting point of any world that truly wants to be considered human.

John Paul II was the Pope of Life, and it is no coincidence that after his death, the grace most received by sterile parents who asked for his intercession was to be able to have a child. Dozens of letters arrived at the Postulator's Office which expressed the hope of receiving this grace, and later to give thanks for the birth of a child.

Many times throughout his pontificate we heard John Paul II "cry out" in defense of the human being. An unforgettable cry was that which we heard in 1981, in the land of Pope John XXIII. While Italy was preparing for the referendum that would result in the legalization of abortion, he asked, loudly calling to the faithful congregated at the threshold of the Sotto il Monte, among strong winds and impressive lightning bolts: "Is it lawful for us men to take a life from an innocent human being, for whom Christ has given his life?" The pontiff added: "If the right to assassinate man when still in the mother's womb is granted, it will trigger a decline of incalculable consequences."

John Paul II was convinced that if human life is not defended, society has no future.

There was not a single trip in which John Paul II did not defend the human being and did not denounce violence, injustice, and discrimination due to race or religion. He repeated constantly that "he wanted to be the voice of those without a voice," whether they were indigenous, laborers, peasants or miners.

On one occasion he commented that when he died, God would ask him to account for how many hours he had spent with the poor and with the powerful. He was convinced that God would judge him by the way in which he addressed the needs of the people who found themselves in circumstances of poverty, hunger and sickness. He became a planetary promoter for the "civilization of love."

During the first trip of his pontificate to Mexico, he wanted to have an encounter with the indigenous people in Oaxaca, to demonstrate his solidarity with one of the most marginalized and forgotten peoples on the planet. In an unforgettable message, the Pope stated that he "wanted to be the voice of those who cannot speak, of those who are silenced, to be the conscience of consciences, and an invitation to action to recover lost time."

On that occasion, and for the first time, the Pope listened to a representative from the indigenous people who with his heart in his hand spoke to him on equal footing. Esteban Hernandez, a Zapotec evangelist, in strong words described the dramatic situation in which the indigenous people lived. He told him:

> We live in worse conditions than that of our animals, relegated to the margins of the sierra, feeling like foreigners in our own land. You said that we, the poor

of Latin America, were the hope of the Church, and look how that hope lives. We have been marginalized in the most inhospitable area of the sierra, the land of our grandfathers. We are lied to, and deceived. We are sad, we eat sad, and live sad.

The Pope responded with words that sounded explosive at the time and which went around the world. Amidst great applause, he said that the Church defends the right to private property. Upon this, however, rests a serious social mortgage so that the possessions serve everyone, and procure the well-being of all. He affirmed that the time had come to undertake innovative and bold transformations. "You should undertake them without expecting more urgent reforms [i.e., from the government]. The peasant and indigenous have a right to aid that is effective, which is neither charity nor crumbs of justice, so that they have access to the development that their dignity as people and children of God deserve." He appealed to the powerful, and asked them to listen to God's voice: "It is not fair, it is not human, it is not Christian to continue with certain situations that are clearly unacceptable," he affirmed.

Since his first trip to Mexico in January of 1979, the Church's commitment to the poor was a subject to which he granted greater importance. He used to say that "it is neither power nor money which the Church should rely on" because it must be on the side of the poor and the oppressed.

For this reason, he looked to have encounters with the most humble in all of his trips; indigenous people, laborers, peasants, and miners among other underprivileged groups. He met with the rich and powerful as well, before whom he declared that someday "the poor nations will judge those peoples who have taken their possessions, assuming an imperialist monopoly of an economic and political supremacy at the expense of others."

## Man of Peace

John Paul II was convinced that peace was not simply the absence of war. During his twenty-six year pontificate he went around the world to affirm that there is no true peace without equality, truth, justice, and solidarity. On dozens of occasions, he told heads of state and governments that the use of arms to settle controversies represents a defeat for mankind. He did not spare any efforts to encourage dialogue, mutual understanding, and respect for differences.

Staff in hand, he traversed the planet to convince mankind of all races, cultures and religions, that there is no peace without justice, no justice without peace, and that true reconciliation amongst peoples where confrontation and enmity exists, is only made possible through true reconciliation with God at the same time. He was never afraid to advocate for justice. He did it before democratic leaders as well as before leftist and rightist dictators. He did so both in rich countries and in the poor ones forgotten by the world. He did so likewise in all the international forums to which he was invited.

One of the most significant characteristics of John Paul II's commitment to world peace was his calling on all religions to work together, starting from their faith in God, for the reconciliation of peoples. One of the most concrete manifestations of this commitment was his summons to the World Day of Prayer for Peace which took place in Assisi, Italy in 1986, to which he invited the leaders of all religions.

It was without a doubt a prophetic decision that revealed

his conviction regarding the importance of all religions in the construction of peace in the world, and which allowed John Paul II to firmly oppose religious fanaticism and wars in God's name. He used to say that "true religion does not have support through terrorism and violence, but looks to promote unity and peace in the human family in every way possible." He was convinced that believers from all religions are called upon to construct peace, leaving aside any forms of intolerance and discrimination.

From the beginning of his pontificate, John Paul II showed himself to the world as a man of peace, as a mediator among the peoples. He conducted his first mediation during "the Beagle conflict," a controversy between Chile and Argentina over the Beagle Channel region.

John Paul II felt compelled to intervene between the two military governments at the time. He sent Cardinal Antonio Samore as his ambassador to both countries, who achieved a promise of peace as a first victory. Later in 1984, he launched negotiations that resulted in a treaty. John Paul II is recalled in both nations as a blessing, and as the Pope of reconciliation and peace.

His commitment to peace was solid and very definite. In addition to the Chile-Argentina conflict, it is sufficient to recall those that took place between Argentina and Great Britain, the wars in the Balkans, the Persian Gulf and Iraq. Thus, he was regarded throughout his entire pontificate as the Pope or pilgrim of peace. No one has ever spoken more about peace, nor been involved with the history and anguish of the peoples as much as John Paul II.

The Pope, who knew first-hand the horrors of war, and saw how hatred can degrade mankind, made his international commitment for peace an essential point of his mission, and above all a clear manifestation of the hope that encouraged him.

On several occasions he wanted to reach the war zones, considered extremely dangerous, to deliver a message of hope. He went to Ireland; Ayacucho, Peru which was at war with the "People of the Shining Path"; Colombia, ravaged by guerrilla warfare; El Salvador, going through a civil war; Argentina and Great Britain, officially at war over the Falkland Islands, to mediate in their conflict.

Since 1982 he indicated he wanted to visit Lebanon. Each year he repeated the same, but the country was at war. In 1989, and with great courage, he announced to the world that he would go to Lebanon, because the Syrians were committing a true genocide. He was unable to achieve it at that time, but anyone who was willing to travel to be in the middle of the bombing in order to express solidarity with a martyred people, fostered a sense of hope and security in them. The same would happen years later in Sarajevo, martyred by violence just as much. The image of the Pope celebrating Mass in a snow storm, experiencing terrible cold before an altar at which side a Christ mutilated by a grenade had been placed over a white sheet, a symbol of all men, women, and children, war victims among Serbs and Bosnians, was unforgettable.

How could one ever forget that the Pope, already very ill, pronounced one of his most impacting messages against war, namely, to avoid the invasion of Iraq, from his private study's balcony.

One Sunday while praying the *Angelus*, the Pope improvised by asking the participants in the conflict to listen to him, because he knew what war was about; he had lived through the horrors of World War II and knew full well that war was never a solution; quite the contrary. In an effort to prevent the United States and their allies from invading Iraq, John Paul II unleashed the Vatican's diplomacy. It was his last international battle to which he consecrated his remaining strength. He sent his ambassadors to speak with those involved, from President George Bush to Saddam Hussein, but his voice was not listened to by the conflict's protagonists. He was however, listened to by the citizens of the world who, moved by the hope that John Paul II instilled in them, began to oppose the war. There had never before been such a large wave of protests on a global scale.

## Man of Forgiveness

John Paul II was convinced that forgiveness was not a synonym of weakness but of strength; a "need" to eliminate all forms of violence and rancor from the personal and collective conscience, to promote "reconciliation" in truth, justice and charity. To him, forgiveness does not undermine the individual; to the contrary, it leads towards a more realized and enriched humanity.

The clearest example of his forgiveness and charity towards his fellow man was when in 1981 he forgave his aggressor, Turkish terrorist Ali Agca. His secretaries, Monsignor John Magee and now Cardinal Stanislaw Dziwisz, narrated that at the moment the attack occurred, John Paul II believed that a bomb had exploded, and that when he saw blood on his finger and on the sash over his tunic, he thanked God for having granted him the grace of having spilled his blood at the Vatican, precisely on the day of the Feast of the Virgin of Fatima. He was very much aware of the significance of the attack's having taken place on that day. He lived his entire convalescence with a spirit of gratitude to the Lord for having allowed him to suffer for the Church. The same way that Jesus did on the cross, he immediately forgave his aggressor.

According to Monsignor Magee, the attack had an enormous influence over the way in which he carried out his ministry. He became more contemplative, like someone who has felt the palpitations of Jesus' wounds on the cross. At the same time he became stronger, more self-confident. From his perspective, Cardinal Stanislaw Dziwisz, his secretary during forty years, affirmed that he never heard John Paul II speak with rancor about the aggressor who had attempted to kill him. He even wrote him a letter, which he did not want published, that said: "How can we present ourselves before God, if we cannot reciprocally forgive each other here on Earth?"

One of his pontificate's most prophetic initiatives was the call to the purification of memory as part of the Jubilee of 2000. The motivation was clear; he asked for courage and humility from those who called themselves Christians to acknowledge the faults they had committed.

The day of forgiveness was celebrated on March 12, 2000. That day's liturgy was called "Confession of Faults and Petition for Forgiveness." It was the first time that a Pope led a solemn ceremony dedicated to the recognition before God, of faults committed, past and present, by the members of the Church. Those who lived that moment were aware that it was a historic event.

There were seven pleas for forgiveness raised under Michelangelo's Dome. John Paul II wanted a plea for the purification of the Christian memory so that the Jubilee would became a true motive for conversion. It was Cardinal Joseph Ratzinger's turn to confess the faults of members of the Church, who in the name of the faith and morals, resorted to non-evangelical methods in their duty to defend liberty; abuses perpetrated against the people of Israel; faults committed against love; the rights of the peoples; peace; respect for peoples' cultures and religions. Forgiveness was also asked for faults committed against women's dignity, humanity, and those who impacted people's fundamental rights. John Paul II also wanted forgiveness to be asked not only for the sins of the past, but for those in the present, and for the responsibility of Christians in today's world.

John Paul II's historic gesture was not only a petition for forgiveness. He offered forgiveness to those who have attacked, persecuted, and martyred Christians, past and present. According to the Pope, the purification of the memory and reconciliation were indispensable for Christians to be able to enter the third millennium as more credible witnesses. His cry still resounds in our ears:

> No more contradictions with clarity in the service of the truth; never more any gestures against the communion of the Church; never more offenses against any people; never more any resources to support a logic of violence; never more discriminations, exclusions, oppressions, disdain for the poor and the least of us.

He knew how to ask for forgiveness in his private life. He asked for forgiveness when he recognized having made a mistake. His collaborators have indicated that on several occasions when the Pope realized he had made a mistake, he admitted it and asked for forgiveness without being ashamed.

## Man of Ecumenical Dialogue

One of the most recognized and appreciated characteristics of John Paul II's pontificate was the promotion of ecumenism and dialogue with other religions. To have been born in a country that was a peaceful oasis of tolerance and coexistence among peoples of different ethnicities and religions for centuries, one in which everyone's right to practice their creed freely was recognized (despite its tumultuous history, there were never wars over religion in Poland), made young Karol develop an openness and respect for others in his homeland.

> During the beatification process I had beautiful encounters with representatives from various Christian communities and members of other religions. Some of these encounters will forever remain in my heart. They are small icons that reveal the open hearted wish for the unity of Christians and the coexistence of all men of goodwill that beat inside John Paul II's chest.
>
> I will never forget Patriarch Bartholomew's warm and friendly reception. I recall his tone of voice when he told me about his diverse encounters with John Paul II. He remembered when in 2004 John Paul II returned the relics from St. Gregory of Nazianzus and St. John Chrysostom during his visit to Constantinople, and the day he gave him a chalice to celebrate the Eucharist in the hope of reaching full unity. The Patriarch appreciated it very much, and decided not to use it until being able to share it in celebration with the Pope. *Monsignor Slawomir Oder*

In his ecumenical haste, John Paul II visited countries of Orthodox majorities, such as Rumania and Bulgaria:

> To Patriarch Teoctist, chief of the Romanian Orthodox Church, John Paul II was a good man and a saint, with a heart full of evangelical zeal, attentive to the spiritual and material needs of Christians, generous in supporting the Church's mission by all means possible and within the context of a real communism.
>
> *Monsignor Slawomir Oder*

John Paul also visited countries with Protestant majorities. Lord Carey, Primate of the Church of England, saw in John Paul II a man devoted to the defense of man and his dignity, as well as of those fundamental values that no Christian could renounce. To him, he was a man of great cultural and spiritual strength, full of passion for Christians. He always cherished as a very special gift, a pectoral cross that the Pope donated to him, in the hope of communion with the sacraments and unity.

One of the most moving aspects of Karol Wojtyla's life was his friendship with Jerzy Kluger, a childhood friend from Wadowice, where a very important Jewish enclave was located.

Their friendship lasted a lifetime. Jerzy, the only survivor from his family, went to live in Rome during the Council years, where he once again met his friend, Archbishop of Cracow at the time. Years later he would see him again, as Pope.

Jerzy Kluger, who was one of the witnesses during the beatification process, told me that when John Paul II visited Rome's synagogue in 1986, becoming the first Pope to do so, it was not the first time he had done it. In 1936 or 1937, Jerzy's father had invited young Karol and his father to Wadowice's synagogue for the visit of David Kussawiecki, a famous religious singer.

Mr. Kluger also spoke about the emotion he felt when his friend returned the religion notebook that young Karol had kept hidden when the Nazis occupied Wadowice, and Jerzy had to leave.

> After John Paul II's death, I found that notebook as a relic in Houston's Holocaust Museum. For me it was a very emotional experience to see it there as a symbol of the bond between Karol Wojtyla and his Jewish friend.
>
> I also remember my encounter with a Jewish woman in Rome who told me that she suffered from the death of two fathers: the first, when her natural father passed away, and the second when the Pope passed away. *Monsignor Slawomir Oder*

His approach to the various Christian realities and to representatives from other religions was the by-product of John Paul II's ecclesial thinking, but it was also an imperative from his heart. To be able to understand his feelings and the motivations behind his most profound gestures, it is indispensable to read his spiritual diary.

Immediately after having been elected Pope, he wrote in his diary: "Everything had been prepared and preceded by suffering. When I became Cardinal, my dearest friend Marian Jaworski lost an arm in a rail accident while on his way to attend a conference in my stead. When I became Pope, another friend of mine, Monsignor Andrea Deskur, suffered an ictus. *Debitor factus sum!*"

To Karol Wojtyla, the awareness of the grace obtained

through the suffering of people closest to him became a commitment and a debt he must repay.

His heart could not be indifferent to the suffering of his friend Jerzy, who lost his entire family in the Auschwitz concentration camp, to the Holocaust and the suffering of any innocent victim from hatred and evil.

His awareness of the debt he had to repay paved the way for his participation with and approach to people, to restoring bonds and bridges over and above any religious, cultural and social differences. First and foremost this participation was demonstrated through the unconditional condemnation of any and all forms of anti-Semitism as something completely contrary to Christians.

The theological dimension of the suffering and the obligations that derive from it, represent one of the most important characteristics of John Paul II's contributions to the establishment of relationships among people. He wanted to make sure that the blood spilled by innocents was never forgotten, and that it represented a calling to new generations to assume responsibility before history to free themselves from all hatred and prejudice towards those who belong to different cultures and religions.

During his trip to the Holy Land in 2000 and his encounter with the rabbis, the Pope advocated for all parties to overcome their prejudices, and openly and fully recognize the patrimony that both Christians and Jews share. In the "Land of Jesus" he repeated he what he had said during his visit to Rome's synagogue when he called the Jews "our older brothers." He expressed the hope that Christians would recognize that the Jewish people's religious heritage is part of their faith, and that the Jewish people would also recognize that the Church totally condemns anti-Semitism in all its forms as it stands in radical opposition to Christian principles. He added: "We must cooperate to build a future in which there is no anti-Jewish sentiment among Christians and no anti-Christian sentiment among the Jewish people."

One of the clearest manifestations of his conviction that addressing the suffering of victims of racial hatred represents a commitment to our contemporary world is found in the message he sent as part of the sixtieth anniversary of the liberation of the Auschwitz concentration camp on January 15, 2005.

In this message, written shortly before his death and which can be considered his spiritual testament regarding the Holocaust, the Polish Pope affirmed that one should never give in to ideologies that justify the possibility of trampling human dignity over differences in race, skin color, language or religion.

However, John Paul II also mentioned that in the middle of so much evil, there were heroic manifestations of adherence to good on the part of prisoners who demonstrated love towards their fellow man and their executioners.

The Pope wrote: "They behaved this way because of their love of God, or in the name of the highest spiritual values. Thanks to this attitude, a truth that is constant in the Bible was imposed: 'although mankind is capable of evil acts, sometimes of enormous proportions, evil will not have the last word. Love can prevail in suffering's abysses.' The testimony of that love, which emerged in Auschwitz, cannot be forgotten. It must unceasingly awaken consciences, eliminate frontiers, and exhort peace."

It was also very significant that he recalled in his message Elio Toaff, Rome's rabbi, with whom he had established a deep friendship.

To John Paul II, to do good to others and contribute to a

better world based on justice and fraternity, represents the most profound and noble manifestation of respect possible towards those who have suffered as a result of human evil.

On many occasions, and from declarations from witnesses who participated in the beatification process, this phrase was heard: "He looked at me and I felt that he saw something more; he saw in me the image of the God he loved."

That spirituality and theological sensibility were precisely the foundation upon which John Paul II's ecumenical and inter-religious efforts were based. On one hand he felt himself being the debtor of love and goodwill and on the other, as one who contemplates God's image in his fellow man. John Paul II's approach to people was always based upon the framework of cordiality and friendship. There were no shortages of extraordinary efforts to overcome barriers based on prejudice, or misunderstandings accumulated over the course of several centuries. It would suffice to remember the World Day of Prayer that took place in Assisi, Italy in 1986, to which he invited the leaders of all religions to pray for peace. Throughout his entire pontificate, the Pope affirmed that God can never be the motive behind any conflict. He asked of Jews and Muslims to work together to achieve a better world, with greater justice and peace.

John Paul II was the first Pope to ever enter a mosque, and was the man who advocated in favor of joint collaboration between Christians and Muslims to avoid new conflicts of religious origin, and confrontations between the two civilizations.

When I travelled to Egypt to listen to testimony from various representatives of the Coptic Church, they told me that the Muslim community had admired and respected John Paul II as a man who knew how to build bridges. One of the bishops from the southern part of the country told me that in almost all the homes of Muslim friends that he visited, he had seen a picture of John Paul II, whom they considered a father figure. Upon his death, Egypt declared three days of national mourning.     *Monsignor Slawomir Oder*

John Paul II's trip to Morocco in 1985 is a memorable one. It was the first papal visit to a Muslim country, and there the Pope had an extraordinary encounter with their youth at a stadium in Casablanca. Sixteen years later he would become the first Pope to enter a mosque in Damascus, Syria. In all his encounters with the Muslim world, the Pope highlighted the common values and beliefs that could represent a starting point to collaborate for peace and goodwill. While inside the mosque in Damascus, the Pope affirmed that "the encounter with God through prayer is the nurturing that our souls need." In 2002, during his visit to Kazakhstan, he demonstrated the Catholic Church's respect for the true Islam, the Islam that prays and knows how to be in solidarity with others. "Hatred, fanaticism, and terrorism profane God's name and disfigure mankind's image," he stated.

Above all, John Paul II advocated for religious and cultural dialogue with Islam. He lamented: "It is bitterly ironic that in a word so framed by violence, even some of the worst conflicts are between believers who adore the same God; consider Abraham, a holy patriarch, and look to follow Sinai's law." He was always opposed to the world's "resorting to violence in the name of religion." It is for this reason that on several occasions he reaffirmed the appreciation that Christians have for Muslims, whose faith in God contributes to the construction of a new human family. "Adoring the only God, creator of us all, encourages us to intensify our future and reciprocal efforts to learn about each other, and walk together on a pathway to reconciliation. By renouncing all forms of violence as a way to resolve differences, the two religions will be able to offer a sign of hope to the world."

The large presence of leaders from diverse religions at John Paul II's funeral was the best demonstration of what he was able to achieve in life, and of the bridges of dialogue that he had built.

# 4 Thanks and Testimonials

As happened after John Paul II's death, and following his beatification, many letters continued to arrive at the Postulator's Office, coming from the faithful all around the world that told about the graces received, which they considered true miracles due to the intercession of Blessed John Paul II.

The Postulator's Office then assumed the charge of analyzing the multiple cases in search of the miracle that might lead to John Paul II's canonization. There were several interesting cases that warranted an investigation.

One of the first cases that "smelled" like a miracle was that of an Italian gentleman who loved to snow ski and take long strolls in the mountains. He had been operated on because one of his heart valves was not functioning and had been substituted by that of an animal. Everything was going well at the beginning, and his prognosis was good. However, shortly after the intervention, the first symptoms of aortic valve insufficiency began to appear, and a new substitution was planned. The gentleman was very worried and discouraged as a result of the first operation's failure. The night before the second intervention, following an invitation from a nun he had encountered casually, he began to pray to John Paul II, asking for his intercession. He told him that he had also loved the mountains and to snow ski and that John Paul II would understand his wish to recover and return to the mountains.

Hours before the second intervention was scheduled to begin, the doctors realized that the valve was functioning perfectly. Everything had returned to normal. Upon being released from the hospital, the gentleman wrote to the Postulator's Office to express his gratitude to John Paul II and tell the story about what had happened. It was decided to go further into the case but unfortunately, and according to the expert involved, it was learned that the instruments used to determine the condition of the valve were not adequate and therefore added a small margin of doubt; therefore they could not proceed further.

Several weeks later, another interesting case arrived at the Postulator's Office. It was about a very dramatic story that took place in Italy. In mid April 2011, a little girl was born with cardio-respiratory problems, prompting the need to hospitalize her in the neonatology section along with two other children. A septicemia epidemic emerged which resulted in the death of the other two children. On the eve of John Paul II's beatification, the little girl herself was gravely ill, thus the doctors told the parents to prepare for the worst. They decided to ask for John Paul II's intercession precisely on the day of his beatification. On the morning of May 1, the girl went through a crisis from which she was not expected to recover. However, at the end of the beatification ceremony, her condition suddenly improved. She began to get better, and at the end of the day she was fine. She was able to return home a few days later. The girl's grandmother sent the case to the Postulator's Office but, because of the death of the two children, the documentation about what had happened ended up in the hands of the police who were tasked with investigating the two children's deaths. The documentation was obtained many months later but it was not possible to demonstrate that it was a miraculous healing. The girl might have simply reacted positively to the proper treatment, and the two children who died were probably more fragile than she.

Another case that had the inkling of a miracle was that of a Lebanese girl, the daughter of Orthodox Christian parents. During the last weeks of gestation, the presence of fluid in the girl's vital organs was detected, which represented a serious threat to her health. The fluid did not disappear after her birth. The girl's uncle, a Catholic priest, decided to ask for John Paul II's intercession. After only a few hours, the fluid disappeared and the organs began to function properly.

The Postulator's Office had two internationally renowned experts study the background of the case. Unfortunately there was no unanimity of opinion about what had transpired. Once again the Office decided to wait for a clearer case. This one finally arrived from Costa Rica.

To many of his collaborators, John Paul II was an intercessor long before Pope Francis officially recognized his sanctity.

Monsignor Alfred Xuereb, one of Pope Francis' current secretaries, began to pray to him immediately after his death. During difficult moments, he would go to the Vatican grottos, and kneel before his tomb. On several occasions he asked for his intercession on behalf of relatives and friends. A couple whom he married could not bear children. The gynecologist told them that the probabilities of her becoming pregnant were minimal. They both prayed to John Paul II. The Monsignor invited them to the grottoes and there he celebrated Mass for both them and a sister of hers who had already suffered two spontaneous miscarriages. "A few weeks later she called me: both were expecting a child, and ultimately both gave birth without issues," narrated Monsignor Xuereb. He also remembers that a couple had arrived from Malta, his country of origin, the day of John Paul II's beatification. Their daughter had experienced a very difficult pregnancy and after nine months, both her twins had been born dead. After this devastating loss, they prayed to John Paul II. A short time later, she became pregnant once again, and this time gave birth to a girl. They had come to the beatification to give thanks, not only for the birth of their granddaughter, but also for the healing of a lady who had overcome serious health problems after praying to John Paul II.

A relative of Monsignor Xuereb's, who could not bear children, had become pregnant with triplets after undergoing fertility treatments. On the fourth month of pregnancy she began to have birth pains. She was on the verge of death. Her brother called the Monsignor in the middle of the night. They both began to pray and to ask for John Paul II's intercession. The young lady was safe; she had to remain in bed through the rest of her pregnancy, but in the end gave birth to her three children.

There is no doubt in Monsignor Xuereb's mind that John Paul II is a man of God who intercedes from Heaven. To him he is not a saint only today after the miracle was acknowledged; he always showed his sanctity during the years the Monsignor worked with him as Prelate of the Antechamber. "Only a holy man could have had the kind of strength and humility to present himself with such speaking problems, when saliva would always pour down the left side of his face, without fearing that it might suffocate him."

Beyond the information about possible miracles, the thousands of letters that arrived from all over the world at the Postulator's Office, or were left on his tomb in St. Peter's, the culmination of thousands of pilgrims' visits speak volumes about the relationship between John Paul II and men, women, young people and children from all continents and social conditions. The common denominator of all of those letters was the conviction that John Paul II was a saintly man, and that the cause to canonize him would only put an official seal to the sanctity that they already felt within themselves. Upon reading all of those messages, one must conclude that, nine years after his death, John Paul II is living still. People continue to have a dialogue with him as if he were alive. They felt his company when he was alive, and they also feel his presence now that he is no longer around. They address him as a friend, a father, not only to ask him for a healing, but also to be able to succeed in an exam, to find employment or a partner, for reconciliation in a family, and to save a marriage.

The letters speak about the people who wrote them, but also about the humanity that John Paul II knew how to manifest throughout his pontificate.

We have selected several testimonies that reflect the extraordinary relationship that remains alive and that time will hardly be able to erase, as well as to the power of his intercession to grant the grace that the faithful all around the world do not cease to ask him for.

> I have always had a special soft spot for Pope John
> Paul II; he always inspired so much confidence,
> so much love, so much peace that when he passed
> away I felt great pain in my heart, in my soul, like
> many millions of people around the world (I forgot
> to add that mine is a very active Catholic family).
> Crying for him, my mother and I told each other

that by his being absent we felt as if we had become orphans. The feeling of loneliness was such that, although Pope Benedict whom we currently have is a great Holy Father, he has not been able to fill the void that John Paul II left on his march to the Father.                                      *young 32-year-old Spanish woman*
*Mexico City, December 24, 2011*

༉

Dear Sir,

During 2010 and 2011 I have been undergoing treatment for bladder cancer that metastasized to one of my lungs. Since last May 17 there has been news about my condition improving, confirmed by follow up analysis, the last having taken place on November 11, 2011.

From the beginning, I put my health under Pope (now Blessed) John Paul II's care, and when my condition took a turn for the worse on February 2011, we intensified our prayers to achieve a miraculous healing, especially because the medical prognosis was very bad (the practitioner indicated that therapy would only serve to "give you more time").

In April of this year my wife started a "prayer chain" in which family members, friends and acquaintances have participated, each of them from their own location but all of them beginning at nine o'clock in the evening; we put emphasis in asking that the children pray, always passing around the approved prayer to ask for favors through John Paul II's intercession.

From a medical perspective I have received the best of treatment; however, I am certain (and I have shared this with both my family and my physicians) that my healing is a favor granted through John Paul II's intercession, even though the necessary examinations and medical oversight must continue.

With these lines I express my gratitude to God, in the hope that they may be useful in the canonization process. Thanks to my wife's diligence, along with this letter I am including a medical chronology of my case which is fully documented.   *Cordially, Juan Pablo*

❧

Good morning,

My name is Inmaculada. I am thirty-four years old and live in the Jerez de la Frontera, Cadiz Province. I am an early education teacher in a religious school and my husband Javier has a small landscaping business. We have three children; Curro, 5 years old; Blanca, three years old; and Nachete, four months old. We are Catholic but have lived our faith very lethargically. First of all I must say that I have dared to write this letter because I promised John Paul II that, in exchange for his returning my son to me alive ,I would do so; and since that's what happened, I find myself compelled to tell the story.

It all began with my third pregnancy; I was expecting a boy at the beginning of April, 2012. The pregnancy was perfect, periodic exams with my lifelong gynecologist with nothing out of the ordinary. It was early morning on a Holy Tuesday when I gave birth to a boy. He weighed 4.3 kilograms and measured 53 centimeters, a beautiful and healthy boy as all the doctors had predicted.

Within forty-eight hours I went home with my third and perfect child since the birth was fast and without complications. Days went by and my son was growing and gaining weight normally. A friend of mine who worked at the Health Center transferred me there since the previous one was too far away, and made an appointment for a baby health control checkup; normally the first checkup takes place within a month of birth, but mine was scheduled within twenty-two days. When we arrived for the checkup, his pediatrician began to examine him and took three seconds; he told us: "I am noticing something strange, go to urgent care to have an electrocardiogram done and come back with the results."

Later on the pediatrician told us that in reality she did not hear anything abnormal, it was a gut feeling, something inside warned her that something strange was happening. When we arrived at urgent care they began to perform an electrocardiogram and measure the level of oxygen in his blood; they used several cables since the results were indicating around 70%, which made the medical staff believe the cables were faulty. The boy started to cry and his skin began to look pale. When they performed the electrocardiogram they told us that he had transposition of large blood vessels, which was not compatible with life. If he had been alive for twenty-two days it was because he had a great orifice between the two ventricular walls where the blood is oxygenated. It seemed incredible that he did not display any symptoms until that very moment when he started to become cyanotic (blue). We were sent to Seville by ambulance; we did not know what was happening and the gravity of the situation; when we arrived at the Virgen del Rocio Hospital, the neonatal medical staff was waiting for us inside the intensive care unit. The entire personnel kept repeating the same phrase: he is past the age. They explained that to gain time, they would try to open the boy's "ductus" with prostaglandin, and told us that the operation had to be performed within the first three weeks of life because the heart could not resist any longer. That same evening my son went to intensive care; he was dying. This was on Tuesday April 24; on Wednesday we were told that the "ductus" procedure was not working and that they would need to operate on Friday since the surgeons only operated on Mondays, Wednesdays, and Fridays. On Thursday morning we were told that they only operated on urgent cases and that his was a rescue operation because they did not believe that he would survive past that night. I lived my son's agony: I saw how his life was slowly ebbing away; he was becoming colder and paler and in his eyes he was asking me to let him go. A coworker of mine gave my husband a holy card with an image of the Divine Mercy, which I was not familiar with much less its relationship with John Paul II. When he gave it to me I began to read the prayer and by coincidence

I saw it was precisely His hour: three o'clock in the afternoon. And that the previous Sunday had been His Sunday. I put the holy card in my son's incubator and spoke to the surgeon because his surgical team was not there (only the emergency team was available) and that unfortunately I had to conform to that. I prayed to the Divine Mercy to help me. Within a short while the surgeon came back very emotional to tell me that his team had learned about the operation and, even though they were off duty attending a fair in Seville, they were on their way back to operate on Nachete. They took my son into surgery on April 26 at 4:30 P.M., and at 8:30 P.M. the surgery was over. It was a very complicated and risky procedure, but it turned out well. The most difficult part was yet to come, to wait for his left ventricle to respond. On April 27, when we went in to see him we were told he was not doing well. I noticed that the Divine Mercy holy card was missing, and my husband told me that it had been left in the operating room. A great anguish inside of me told that my son was dying; I knew it; I knew that he needed a miracle.

Back at the school where I work, everyone started a "novena" to John Paul II, and told me to do the same. I sent the picture of John Paul II along with his prayer to all my friends, even on Facebook, I had nothing to lose and asked everyone to pray, the more people the better. At 1:00 P.M. in the afternoon we were told to bid him goodbye; that his heart was not responding, and he was experiencing many tachycardia episodes, one of which could result in an angina. He could then be connected to an artificial heart but they would only have to disconnect it later. They would give him a window of two hours to monitor his condition. I prayed with all my strength and told John Paul II: "I commend my son into your arms; please return my son to me alive and well, and I will give my testimony for you to become saint." At that moment, 1000 girls prayed to John Paul II simultaneously, and hundreds of people who had never prayed before started doing so to help save my little boy. At 9:00 P.M. we went upstairs to see him. The Divine Mercy holy card was once again at his bedside, next to John Paul II's picture which someone had placed there. The doctors were astonished as his left ventricle had started to function again; he was still gravely ill, but not terminally so. From that moment on the miracle was palpable, something that could not be explained: one day his kidneys stopped functioning, and I told everyone; please pray so that he can urinate, and the next day he could. On May 1, my son was out of danger, and removed from the respirator, which can normally be very complicated. He was breathing normally. On Sunday May 6, he was transferred to the neonatal intensive care unit; already out of danger, he acquired an infection but was fine the next day. His recovery was amazing. Twelve days after surgery he began to breast feed and was in perfect health. Twenty-two days after having been admitted to the hospital, we were home. The doctors and nurses truly believed it was a miracle as they did not have an explanation.

During this entire process, many people who were

lukewarm to the faith, beginning with us, became closer to God; many people told me: "Inma, I have never prayed, but am doing so now for your son, because I am seeing that prayer does help as your son is recovering."

There was also another case of a couple from Conil de la Frontera, my husband's hometown, who called us because the woman was five months pregnant and had been diagnosed the same as our son. She had been advised that he would not survive, and to abort the pregnancy. We explained to them that this was not true, that once the baby was born he could have a simple surgical procedure, and everything would be fine. Today that child is home after surgery and in perfect health.

Additionally, a prayer group was formed over the Internet by mothers from the school during my son's convalescence at the hospital, which prayed the Divine Mercy chaplet. This group continues to grow and is attracting people who have gone a bit astray from God.

My son is at home, having recuperated completely and without any complications; according to the doctors, they did not expect him to survive, much less not have any complications. They only gave him a two hour window to live, within which thousands of people prayed for a miracle.

*Jerez, Spain, August 20, 2012*
*Inmaculada*

It has been over one year since I began an unbroken "novena" to John Paul II. The intention was because of one of my children, whose girlfriend over the last seven years had changed him, and pushed him apart from our family. Yesterday my son told me that he had finally broken up with his girlfriend. I know in my heart that this happened thanks to John Paul II, because I put my son in his hands every day for him to decide what was best. Yesterday I received the answer to my prayers. After so much time talking to John Paul II, I will continue with the "novena" to help others who may need it, always knowing that he always listens to us, no matter how desperate our intentions are. I am certain that my faith in him made it possible for my son to start a new life, surrounded by the family that loves him dearly.

*Regards, Alejandra (Argentina)*

☙

I am thirty years old, a native of Tamaulipas, Mexico, and have been married for one year and a half. Months ago, last year, I had a dream where I saw John Paul II and myself in the latter stages of my pregnancy. After that dream I prayed to John Paul II for his intercession, to allow me to be a mother someday, because to me that dream was a sign. A few months later John Paul II's relics came to Tamaulipas as part of a multi-city tour, and I went to see them. Ten days later I learned that I was pregnant, that John Paul II had interceded for me before God. I am actually twelve weeks pregnant and continue to ask for his intercession for my baby to be born healthy this coming August, God willing. I hope that my testimony is of value to add to so many others.

☙

Good afternoon,

I am Colombian and wish to share my testimony:

A priest gave the John Paul II novena to my daughter, who in turn wanted to give it to a cousin who had recently lost a baby. We wished for his intercession, for God to grant her a new baby. Before it reached its destination, I prayed the "novena" (to John Paul II) to ask for my heavenly Father's intervention on behalf of a sister of mine, 55 years of age, whose name is Clara Ines. She was unemployed, living in a bedroom from which she was about to be evicted, and had nothing to eat. Then, after I finished the "novena," three job offers came in. She did not want to accept any of them, until she finally made a decision. The bosses are very good people. Additionally, her son, who was also unemployed, found a job. Although it sounds like a simple favor, it is important to remember that it is very difficult if not impossible for people older than thirty years of age to find employment in Colombia.

Other people have prayed our "novena," and when they have they have received benefits from it, but we are writing about the closest one to us. I am grateful that you have listened to my testimony.

*Marlene (Colombia)*

☙

By praying to His Holiness, Blessed John Paul II, I have been granted two wishes that I had asked for regarding my son and godson, both of whom were unemployed and desperate about not finding anything after an eight month search. Finally, and thanks to the Blessed John Paul II, both of them found good jobs. We wanted to communicate this and give thanks.

*Sincerely, Marisa*

❧

Dear Monsignor Slawomir Oder:

I am sending this communication to your Excellency as a gesture of my respect and gratitude to our Holy Father John Paul II, because through his intercession we received a great miracle and grace without equal for our family. This past July 13, 2012, my father, a man eighty years old, was at the Medica Sur hospital, suffering from acute pneumonia. Around ten o'clock in the morning he suffered a respiratory failure; my mother and I prayed to His Holiness to intercede for us and for our Lord to let him be with us a little longer. This is exactly what happened; the doctors were able to resuscitate him, and after several days of intensive therapy, his condition improved, thanks to God's infinite mercy, and our beloved John Paul II's intercession. I made a promise to John Paul II that I would write and send this testimony to Rome, as part of the cause for his canonization. This is why I am addressing your Excellency.

Hoping that the grace we received serves in the cause of His Holiness John Paul II's being canonized, I am at your service, including the providing of all pertinent information, and wishing God's blessings so you too become a saint. *Maria Teresa (Mexico)*

&

My son was born prematurely by C-section during my wife's 34th week of pregnancy due to intrauterine growth retardation. Upon his birth, the baby was admitted to the pediatric intensive care unit, and despite having received a pulmonary surfactant, my baby's condition worsened over time, to the extent of being in danger of death in the early morning of August 20, 2011. The doctor diagnosed a probable case of intrauterine pneumonia, and the baby remained connected to a respirator for another week.

With great faith in God and asking for the intercession of the Blessed Virgin Mary and Blessed John Paul II, whom I had the pleasure of seeing in Bucaramanga, during his visit to Colombia when I was a child and belonged to the choir that sang the Eucharistic hymn; that same August 20th, our baby was baptized in the intensive care unit by the clinic's senior chaplain.

We have lived our son's recovery day by day from the beginning of this episode (pulmonary dysplasia, patent foramen oval, oxygen dependency); we have relied upon both material and spiritual support from family and friends; we have seen how God has worked in our lives to the point that today we reside in a city with a better climate for our son; I have retained my job with my current employer, teleworking from 400 kilometers away, even when teleworking legislation is just beginning to be enacted in Colombia. We have seen first-hand how God has touched our hearts and worked in our lives. This is why I offer this testimony, because I am totally convinced that both Our Lady and Blessed John Paul II's intercessions have been effective.                                        *Javier (Colombia)*

❧

With appreciation

Every morning I implored the intercession of John Paul II and my prayers were answered: After more than seven years of not being able to get pregnant due to mistakes of my past, thanks to John Paul II and God, today July 31, 2012 I am pregnant. May God care for my baby so that he is born healthy. I will be thirty-seven years old in September 2012, and this is a miracle that God has granted me. Many, many thanks.

*Attentively, Adriana*
*(Ecuador)*

❧

Monsignor Slawomir Oder:

I address you to inform you that my family and I have been through a very difficult period during which, through prayer, I asked for the intercession of John Paul II, the servant of God. I felt comforted by him at all times, always hopeful of his help, and this enabled me endure those difficult moments. Everything turned out well with the help of the medicine and John Paul II to whom I prayed. I will always continue to pray for his intercession before God and for my son's health to continue to be as good as it has up to this point.

The purpose of my letter is to send you information in writing about the miracles that His Holiness John Paul II carried out on my behalf.

The first and most important one that I want to share with you is that three weeks ago, Blessed John Paul II along with the Virgin of Guadalupe helped me make one of my dreams come true: to buy a house. I asked the Blessed so much for this miracle to become a reality. He helped me from the beginning of the process through the end. I live in Boston, MA, USA and have lived here for sixteen years. I saw this process so distant because the price of property here is much higher that in my country of origin. I am very grateful for all the help and unconditional support I received as I went through this process.

Another miracle I want to mention in this letter is how he helped me during my two years of study to complete my Master's Degree Program. Every day I asked the Blessed to enlighten me in my studies and to be able to continue to perform in my job because I was also working full time during that period as well. It was a very difficult time, but well worth it. I completed the program and graduated in May of this year.

Additionally, the Blessed, along with the Virgin of

Guadalupe, helped me win a court case concerning an accident I suffered in Puerto Rico. The case lasted two years but with the Virgin of Guadalupe's help, I was able to win the case and, with the judgment award, pay part of my university study program.

The process to receive all these miracles has been difficult. I am very grateful to the Blessed for his help throughout all these years. I pray to him for my family every day, for friends who live troubled lives, for my job, and to help me find a good man who will respect me for the rest of my life, and to make another one of my dreams come true: to be a mother.

❦

It was April 2011, and my life appeared to collapse because my husband had fallen into a deep depression and did not seem to care about anything. He was totally consumed by alcohol. He had started treatment only a few weeks before, but was not taking it well, staying in bed, not wanting to go to work; the medications were keeping him in a sedated state, and triggering sudden mood changes. He would shout at me all the time, throw me out of the house and even threaten to hurt me. I did not know what to do. One day I was invited to attend Mass at a local Church, the Church of the Visitation, and to my surprise they were paying tribute to John Paul II by showing a video that showed a very large image of his sweet face. I immediately felt a strange sensation, between sadness and great faith in him. I knelt and prayed to him to intercede for us to save our family, and for my husband's health. I put my family in his interceding hands, and shortly thereafter things began to change drastically. The treatment has been successful to date, and the sudden mood changes are less frequent; our marriage has been saved, and despite the difficulties, hope has returned to my life. *Ana Carolina*

❦

Dear Monsignor Slawomir Oder:

Forgive me for writing to you as you must be a very busy person, but I wanted to tell you that only two weeks after praying to John Paul II, the throat specialist told our daughter-in-law that her cancer was in remission. How could we not thank God? She had surgery to remove two tumors from her throat, yet there are absolutely no remnants of them today. I also wanted to tell you that I loved John Paul II since the moment he was elected Pope. I followed him everywhere. When I saw his itinerary on TV, I would get up to pray for him. I always prayed, day and night, and dreamed about me shining his shoes, and understood that my prayer had a purpose. I then increased my prayers, and dreamed to be able to go see him in Rome but the Lord did not allow it. When he came to Costa Rica I went to the airport but could not attend the Eucharist because I had a small child, but God knows how much I loved him, how much I prayed for him, and how much I cried when he died. Several days ago I dreamed that I was at the Eucharist with him, and that he extended his hand to me. Imagine the joy when I woke up today. I have a big picture of him in my room and now I can pray to him every morning and evening asking him to intercede for a variety of situations. Monsignor, I pray on behalf of my three sons' marriages, our ten grandchildren's vocations, and for Felipe and Daliana to have a baby.

*Costa Rica*

∾

I want to offer testimony about the help I am receiving by offering my prayers to God, asking for John Paul II's intercession along with Sts. Vicenta Maria Lopez and Vicuña. I began my prayers on June 24, 2011 to ask for help with a very delicate marriage and family situation. I had no more hope but to put this issue in the Lord's hands, because there was no solution that would come from man. This is why I entrusted my entire family (husband, children and myself) to John Paul II and St. Vicenta Maria to put us in our Lord's hands, to intercede for a definite solution to a problem that has existed for many years; for my family to remain united and become a temple of the Lord; and for my husband to open his heart to Jesus Christ and follow the path of love that He has prepared for us. For these I implored and continue to implore John Paul II, for him, who with so much power transmitted the message of Christ to my life, and reached so many ears and hearts, to also speak to my husband.

Within a few days I began to observe the first signs

of change. Everything develops slowly, not all in one swift moment, but as a process where events begin to occur that get us on the right path. First, my husband partially acknowledged having a problem and decided to seek professional help to try to solve it. Later, he wished to have an encounter with the Lord through his family, for which he proposed the reading of the Bible every Sunday in our home's living room, and convert the room into a chapel for that particular moment. I hope that these developments continue and to share Jesus Christ's way with other families with whom we can get together and live in Him. When this moment occurs, I will once again communicate it.

Thank you.

૭

Hello, my name is Edmundo; I live in Mexico and am writing to you because last January, 2011, I was diagnosed with testicular seminoma tumor. This tumor was surgically removed; however, metastasis occurred. A larger tumor had developed in the retro peritoneum area, for which I had to receive chemo treatment. I received chemotherapy for three months; the treatment ended before Holy Week because I had a PET/CT scan which indicated that the tumor had dissolved. That same exam however, revealed the possibility that another tumor had developed in the mesenteric layer. John Paul II's beatification was coming around that same time. I always loved him very much, and people told me that I should ask him to intercede as more favors were granted when he was being celebrated. This is how I began to ask for his intercession. At the beginning I did, but I also asked for others' intercession, such as St. Teresa of Avila, St. Charbel, and St. Francis, but in this second phase I only asked John Paul II's, because my condition was very serious, and I know that both Jesus and the Blessed Virgin Mary have him very close by. I now know that he interceded for me, for the tumor that was seen coming disappeared from one day to the next without any explanation, and only by Our Lord God's intervention through John Paul II's intercession. To me and many other people, he is already a saint. If you want more information please tell me what I need to do because I want to shout it so that people do not lose hope, especially because of the times we are living here in Monterrey and in Mexico in general, where people live in sadness and anguish.

*Edmundo (Mexico)*

❧

Good afternoon, I want to offer testimony of a beautiful miracle that my family and I received through the Blessed John Paul's intercession.

In February of this year, the daughter that my husband and I expected (I, being six months pregnant) was diagnosed with a serious brain anomaly. The doctors told us many things, all very painful and negative; we were told that our daughter would die in my womb;

that she could be born only to die a few days later, or that she would be born totally deprived of her faculties. Of course after listening to our first physician's diagnosis, we sought many other opinions, which all concurred that the problem was there, and that the gravity could not be ascertained with any degree of certainty. These were very painful months, visiting doctors, hoping that things would improve. During those moments full of anguish and desperation, I received images, medallions, and prayers to the Lord of Mercy, as well as the prayer to ask for John Paul II's intercession. My husband and I decided to pray and put ourselves in God's hands, praying for our daughter with all our hearts each and every day. There were many people who joined our family in prayer, all of them praying to John Paul II, asking for the humanly impossible: for our daughter to be healthy. And then the moment of birth came, and my husband and I were full of hope and faith. Our daughter was born on May 1st of this year, precisely on the day of the Divine Mercy and John Paul II's beatification. She was born just as Mass ended, with no issues. When she was born, all the physicians were waiting to take her to observation immediately after birth. Our daughter is almost one month old now, and is perfect! Thank you Lord Jesus, King of Mercy and thanks to His Holiness John Paul II who interceded on our behalf!! We will never stop giving thanks for this incredible miracle!

John Paul II, I give you thanks for such a beautiful day for the entire Christian community, to soon be able to see you become Saint. Via this note I want to give testimony of my faith and devotion to you. You protected me during my surgery, and were always by my side. I had the privilege of feeling your presence. In gratitude to the protection I received, I always pray to you and ask you to protect the sick. I will always be near you through my prayers.     *Martha (Uruguay)*

❧

Good afternoon. The reason I am contacting you is because I would like to tell you about two experiences that I have had concerning my petitions to John Paul II.

The first was in the month of September of this year, in which I was not feeling well health-wise, with stomach problems. A study revealed that I had an ulcer crater. They wanted to determine if it was bleeding and how much, because I had a lot of discomfort. I was very afflicted. Precisely when I went to church one Sunday, I saw that they were selling small medallions of various saints. I just saw John Paul II's, and when I was paying for it I squeezed it hard with my hand and asked him to help me, because I would undergo an endoscopy the next day and was afraid. When they performed it that Monday, there was no ulcer, only moderate gastritis and pylori bacteria. I was jumping with joy because it would only require a simple therapy.

Another miracle is that yesterday I submitted my work assignment for review, and asked John Paul II to help me again; I prayed to him, and the work was approved. It was the fifth time I had submitted it, but my nerves always betrayed me. I asked him to help and enlighten me and that is exactly what happened. There are more things I need to ask for, because testing will soon follow and I have never been able to pass.

Thank you John Paul II.

☙

Good afternoon, my name is Luz Yaneth; I am thirty-one years old, and am an active Catholic. My family and I have greatly needed a miracle for my brother Luis Ariel, twenty-three years old, who had fallen into drug addiction since he was sixteen and, despite rehab center treatment and intense prayers on our part, could not stop. Eight months ago a friend of mine recommended that I pray the rosary. I dedicated myself to reciting it daily, but the conversion and miracle only took place a few days after I dedicated my daily prayer to John Paul II, and told him: "John Paul II, you who have loved young people so much, help me from heaven with my brother who is being lost, who is dying. Please remind God that He died for him too, to listen to our prayers because He has made my brother intelligent and noble. Tell Him to cure him, save him and free him from addiction." Less than one week later, my brother received a call from a friend of the family to invite him to a spiritual retreat in the seminary at John Paul II City, at a cost of one hundred thirty dollars in Colombian currency.

My brother said that he was not very convinced that it would work, that there was no faith inside of him, and he was without direction or devotion to God. From the first day of prayer, he felt freed and told us about experiencing such joy that he could not stop smiling and crying. Now this young man prays the rosary on a daily basis, attends young Catholic prayer groups, works and meets his obligations, administers his budget well, is committed to be a missionary, and work for Jesus and the Virgin Mary. To me it is a miracle realized with Blessed John Paul II's help. Thank you very much.

Dear friends in the Vatican, I present myself before you: I am José from Uruguay. I address you to tell you about the miracle that John Paul II granted me. For financial reasons, my son could not continue with his studies, as the only place where the career he sought was available was in the Catholic University. When I got up, while drinking "maté" I looked at the image of the Holy Father that I have, and asked him for help with this situation. Two hours before the closing of registration, I received a gratifying telephone call from a friend to tell me that he had obtained a very important discount for my son to be able to attend college. With tears in my eyes and a knot in my throat I looked at John Paul II's image and told him: "Thank you very much Holy Father." Today my son is in his first year of Economics at Uruguay's Catholic University. Through his intercession I ask the picture of the Holy Father John Paul II to help not only my family, but anyone who needs his help.

*José (Uruguay)*

༓

Hello, my name is Monica.

I am from Mexico and my testimony of faith is that I was blessed through our merciful God and the love that John Paul II offered Him. Upon learning that I was pregnant, I asked for my baby's well-being because the conditions in which he was conceived were not the best.

Since I began to read his prayer I felt very comfortable, and with a beautiful inner peace. God and John Paul II were present; I even knew that my baby would be a boy because they told me so. Today I read and will continue to read this prayer, because it has brought me many blessings; it has truly realized great miracles in my life and with the arrival of my beautiful and healthy baby, I entrust him to them every day.

I have a friend whose name is Maritza; she is married and has three children. She's had a cancerous tumor in her head; she was operated on, but the tumor came back. She would once again be operated on, but had to sign documents that indicated she would probably become a paraplegic. The operation took place and she remained in bed in very bad shape. Her husband cared for her for a while, when she began to have convulsions. She and her family began to pray the rosary to John Paul II with a rosary they had borrowed. This rosary was on the Pope's tomb three times, when someone visited Rome two years, six months ago. Maritza was being cared for by her husband during the night. One night she sees a man with a white tunic like that of a priest, and with a ribbon tied around his waist and down to his shoes. She thinks it is her husband, whose name is Jonel, but it could not be him because he had no white clothes, when this man tells her: "Do not be afraid, for you will be cured." He approached her and put his hand on her head. This happened twice, and now she is completely healed. She already has the test results from the Mexico Hospital in San Jose, Costa Rica, where she was operated on and declared healed. Maritza now lovingly cares for her husband, children and home. Please receive my greetings and my request for your blessing. *Soledad (Costa Rica)*

November 24, 2011

Good day. My name is Diego, from Colombia. I had written previously to offer testimony about having received a favor from John Paul II in having rescued me from financial troubles. This time he has listened to my prayers in recapturing the love of the one who will be my future wife. I almost lost her because of my mistakes. During my days of anguish I asked the Holy Father to help me get her back. Within one week and miraculously things got better and all problems were resolved. This was fifteen days ago. Today we are happily together again. Many thanks to Blessed John Paul II.

*Diego (Colombia)*

༝

I would like to tell about the favor I received from Providence, considering Blessed John Paul II the intercessor. I was driving on my way to the school of my sisters Emilia, Paula and Gracia. There was diesel fuel spilled on the road and my car began to slide. I first avoided the vehicles in front of me, and later went against the embankment where one of my car tires exploded; the car bounced and flipped over. After it fell back to a normal position, I realized the situation. I was intact. I got out of the car, checked to see if there was anybody injured or collisions with other vehicles. I mention this because this is a very busy roadway, and schools finished their classes for the day precisely around that time. I verified that indeed there were no injuries to my body, nor any cuts by the broken glass. Nothing! I returned to the car to collect my papers, and the first thing I found was a picture of His Holiness that I always carry in my car to awaken God's presence in me, and my devotion to the Blessed.

I was in Rome during Holy Week 2005, a week

prior to John Paul II's death. I could see him from afar, by the window, when he, with the last of his strength left, gave us his last blessing *urbi et orbi*. And before that, in 2002, I was present for the canonization of José Maria Escrivá de Balaguer. At the end of the Thanksgiving Mass on October 7th, celebrated on his behalf, the Holy Father appeared in St. Peter's Square mounted his Pope Mobile, and when he passed in front of me I could see him face to face. I, a fourteen-year old boy, had climbed over chairs to be able to see him up close; and when the Pope looked at me I became paralyzed. I felt his gaze for a few seconds, and felt a great love for him. I always prayed for his health; and after he passed away I have reached out to him for his intercession several times. *Fernando*

Good afternoon,

I send my testimony regarding what has happened with the petitions I have made to John Paul II. I have been married for four months; I married a person with nervous problems (anxiety, depression), an illness through which I have suffered along with him during our courtship of three years.

On February 20th, my husband had a serious nervous breakdown, in which he became distant and the only thing he was waiting for was for a brother of his to arrive with very strong pills that made him feel better.

My husband had been taking those pills for some

time, and they are very strong; to me it is a drug that one minute makes him feel well, which concerns me because of the negative side effects it could generate later.

During my wedding, I was given a holy card with the image of John Paul II and the Virgin of Guadalupe. That day, seeing how desperate my husband was, reclined on a chair like he was gone, I ran to my room and while crying, asked John Paul II for his intercession with the Virgin of Guadalupe to help me so that I would not see him like that again, to make him healthy, to remove his dependence on that medicine that was so strong and was damaging his body; to never again afflict him because both he as well as I were suffering through his affliction. First thing the next day, a woman arrives at my place of work and we begin to talk. She mentioned not feeling too well but that she was beginning to improve. It turned out that she was suffering from the same affliction as my husband's, and was taking the same strong medication. She went on to tell me: "You know what, buy these vitamins for him. They are natural and will do him well, without any side effects to his body."

Promptly, after leaving work, I went looking for the vitamins, got home and gave them to him. Thanks to John Paul II and the Virgin of Guadalupe; from that day on when I entrusted him to John Paul II, he is fine. He is calm now, and tells me he feels well; thank God. I thank John Paul II greatly for having answered my prayers; I know it was him who listened, and sent this person to give me her advice.

Daily prayers to John Paul II have helped me greatly; my husband and I are and will always be grateful
to him; we are now asking him for us to have a baby,
whose well-being we will entrust to him as well. We
made a promise to him that if it was a boy he would
be named John Paul, and Karol if born a girl. We have
a lot of faith that John Paul II will help us once again.
Many thanks for giving me the opportunity to write
about this great joy that I owe to John Paul II and the
Virgin of Guadalupe.                          *(Mexico)*

ॐ

Last week it rained a great deal here where I live; my
house has been flooded twice, and we were told we
were on the verge of being flooded again. I, along
with two of my sons, read John Paul II's prayer; immediately after, the rain ceased and nothing happened.
I know he must be sanctified, for I particularly have a
great deal of faith in him. Thank You.

*(Tulancingo, Hidalgo, Mexico)*

ॐ

We give thanks to John Paul II from the bottom of
our hearts; he has always accompanied us throughout
our lives with his example; his strength and profound
love gave us courage and the spirit to endure my
husband's lengthy illness. Since 1995 he has suffered
from a grave form of multiple sclerosis.

We always address John Paul II as a good father to

console us in our pain and lead us to God's mystery, and comprehend the meaning of the cross. We have trusted him and have opened ourselves to Christ, accepting his will. *An Italian Couple*

༄

My greetings, respect, and blessings from Venezuela. We are a Catholic family and hereby want to share a testimony with you, a blessing of which we were witnesses in my home. On April 2, 2005, my son cried in his room over the death of God's servant, John Paul II. All of us at home were equally sad about his death. My nine-year-old son, after having been in his room for a long time, came out looking for me still with tears in his eyes, to show me an image that appeared on his bed (it is still there, perfectly clear on a piece of wood). I went to his room and there I could see the image; I confess that I did not know what to do at that moment. In mid-May of this year, and after the Holy Father's beatification, my son suffered from severe tonsillitis. I prayed quite a bit to the Pope for his recovery. Several days later my son healed rapidly, without a doubt thanks to John Paul II and his intercession to our God Almighty. Since that day, not only is the Holy Pope's image on my son's bed, but also the image of our Lady Virgin of the Miracles, who appeared there as well.

I beg of you to please tell me where I can send a picture that supports my aforementioned testimony, or whatever you consider proper. *Karina (Venezuela)*

☙

I prayed that through his intercession, the business where I have worked for the last eight years would reflect on their payroll records, the correct salary I receive; lower salary figures continued to appear constantly, which would seriously and negatively impact my retirement over the long term. It was nearly impossible for my employer to accept to make the correction, as it would result in them having to pay much more into the social security fund.

I prayed to the Blessed with great faith for this need and promised that if he conceded me this favor, I would write to support the cause of his beatification. Shortly after having asked John Paul II for his intercession, I asked my employer (these events occurred in May of 2011) to please solve this problem with payroll and provided details to support my request. The company acknowledged the error without any issues, and made the necessary corrections to their payroll records, retroactive to January 2011.

This meant a lot to me, and I consider it most important, because we are living through an economic crisis, and salaries have not increased in three years. Additionally, throughout my eight years working there, my employer had not acknowledged and accepted my claim to correct their payroll.

I am convinced that Blessed John Paul II's intercession on my behalf made it possible, as he has done by interceding for so many other people.          *Cordially,*
*Margarita*

On September 2nd, it will be a year since I passed through the intensive care unit. I was on the verge of losing my life because of a serious error I had committed: I had pulmonary thromboembolism. On September 2nd I fell asleep but with a lot of effort because it is difficult to sleep in a place where you hear the sound of other patients' monitors thinking that your life is hanging by a thread. I fell asleep asking God to forgive me and return my health which I, by my own doing, had put at risk. I woke up calling out to Karol Wojtyla; at the beginning I did not know who I was calling out to, and later realized it was none other than our beloved and Blessed John Paul II. There my closeness to him began; I simply knew that God had sent a messenger to me, and that he was accompanying me, sinner that I am.

I am totally healed today, in the hope that I will continue to heal my soul and heart for the innumerable sins that I continue to commit, but I know that God loves me and always shows me signs of His love, such a pure form of love that only He can offer. I ask God to grant me His forgiveness, and ask of John Paul II to intercede on my behalf so that I can reach salvation and remedy for my anguish.

Thank you beautiful God and John Paul II. With all my love,                                    *Claudia (Colombia)*

My childhood and adolescence were spent under the sign of Blessed John Paul II. He captivated me from the very first moment. He seemed to look into the deepest point of my soul, as if he knew me from among all of those people; as if I were the only one and he only loved me despite my sins and weaknesses. I did what was possible, and many times the impossible, to follow him, especially during his three visits to Portugal and his several World Youth Jubilees.

He touched my heart many times; he pushed me towards the seminary to belong to the Lord, as he himself belonged to the Lord and the Virgin completely. I resisted: career, success, affections, family, friends, everything turned into an obstacle, each one of them at different times in my life, for me to continue to be what I was: a layman committed to the Church.

However, his last days overcame my resistance; his struggle, his spiritual and physical combat to follow Christ to the cross marked me as if I lived the Gethsemane, as if I followed Christ's path. His death threw all obstacles, my doubts, and my resistance, to the ground. In 2000 I went to Israel, where I had been with Him on the Mount of Beatitudes. There something happened in my heart. In the Primacy of Peter, Jesus asked me: "Do you love me?", and would send me to graze His sheep. I responded that I was afraid, and returned to my life.

With Benedict XVI elected, I continued to search for Christ. I was afraid of not being a good priest, that my sins were a scandal for my smaller brothers; I was totally at the mercy of my own strength, and ignored the power of Grace.

My heart longed to follow that Jesus whom John Paul II preached about, and his beatification was the proof of God's calling in my life. In Rome I have cried for my sins, my silly life, and my idols. I committed myself to Christ, and asked John Paul II to help me. I have known God's Grace as my life's only weapon. To this day I have been faithful in my health, my priestly life, in my love for Christ, to the Virgin, to the Eucharist and the Church.

Now that the Church will inscribe him in the catalogue of saints, I can only ask him: "Please continue to love this poor man who has loved you so much, and continues to love in the heart of Christ the Priest!"

*Pablo (Portugal)*

❧

Since my childhood I was anxious to become a priest. I did not enjoy toys like kids my age; I spent my time building altars; anything that had to do with the Church attracted me. When His Holiness came to Mexico in January 1999, I did not miss the TV transmission of his visit, and was surprised at how people poured out to see him. I was four years old and already wanted to be like him; I looked for anything white to put on my head as a skullcap and climbed onto vehicles thinking they were the Pope Mobile, imparting blessings to everyone, wanting to follow the traveling Pope's example. That is how my childhood continued, doing pilgrimages and celebrating Masses in my own childish way. When John Paul II became seriously ill in 2005, I felt as if someone from my own family was not feeling well.

And on April 2nd of that year, as soon as I woke up I had the feeling that the Pope was going to pass away. I said so to my parents and they replied that it did not appear that anything was going to happen; but at 2:37 P.M. Mexico time, the unexpected occurred: The Pope departed to the House of the Father.

I felt very bad about his death, and even worse about not having met him personally; at the same time I had the certainty that he was now going to be by my side spiritually, and I challenged myself to follow his example and to venerate him with more fervor: I already saw him as a saint.

Years went by and I began to acquire all of the pictures of him that I saw, no matter how large or small they were, because I wanted to have something of him. In 2007 I learned about the work of the Postulation and requested a relic of the Pope; nobody expected that it would ever arrive, but it did; I received a relic *ex indumentum* from Maria Victoria (how emotional I was to receive such a gift!). I continue to want to be like him, to follow his example.

Later, John Paul II granted a miracle to my family by allowing my cousin, named Karol in his honor, to be born. With that I believed that he was really by my side, and that he listened to anything I asked; this prompted my need to follow him even more.

John Paul II's beatification was a great moment for me; even though I could not attend, I did not miss any of the event's activities.

I am convinced that I owe everything to him, because he has always been by my side and has helped me to follow my vocation. When one day Monsignor Oder extended an invitation to me via letter to follow his example as father, pastor, friend and priest, I said to myself: "Why not? I have nothing to lose, and everything to gain," and so here I am following his footsteps.

Because I know that he listens to me, every day I ask him to grant me the grace to be the custodian of one of his relics, and have the certainty that some day I will achieve my goal because he grants me everything I ask of him. *Eduardo Esteban (Mexico)*

❧

Five years ago, and five weeks into my pregnancy I had to be admitted to Moscow Hospital 31 as a result of massive bleeding and the danger of a spontaneous abortion. Doctor Olga Mishieva, the hospital's Chief of Gynecology and Obstetrics, along with Dr. Professor Bragina, wanted to perform an abortion forcefully through surgery; even though the hemorrhage had ceased, they continued to insist on performing an abortion and for me not to tell my husband anything; they said that, because of my age (forty-nine years of age), and it being my first pregnancy, the child would be a monster and would not even survive. I responded that this was impossible, because it is a human being that Divine Providence was granting us, as a result of me asking for it with a lot of faith and for a long time. For this reason, when I became pregnant we consecrated the future baby to the Lord and made a vow to educate him in the Christian faith, in the love of God and our fellow man. And that everything was subject to the Divine and not human will.

Doctor Bragina advised me not to tell my husband anything; to think about it because I had a myoma or uterine fibroid, which was growing faster than the fetus and that the fetus would die soon. I once again responded that I believe that the Lord and the Holy Virgin Mary love us and that I have no secrets from my husband. I quickly called him and told him what was happening. My husband Nicolay went to Moscow's Immaculate Conception Cathedral, where there is a bust of the Blessed John Paul II, and for more than two hours, he knelt and asked for his intercession before the Lord to grant us the grace for our son to be born and to save my life. My husband Nicolay carried a sonogram that they had done on me, and placed it over the Blessed's heart. He was later present at two consecutive Masses at the Cathedral. When he came out of the Cathedral he called me at the hospital and told me with great optimism and joy: "We are not alone, I have felt that everything will be all right; John Paul II will help us. He has heard my prayers." And in reality, after his call I did not feel any more pain and over time the hemorrhage slowly subsided; when Nicolay arrived at the hospital, I already felt very well.

The next day, Monday, the doctor did not want to believe it, and ordered a hormonal analysis to see the levels of the estrogen and progesterone; and it appears that the tests came up with false results twice as pregnancy was not possible with those levels. My husband asked for my blood to be drawn and took it to two different and independent laboratories. The results were identical: a good pregnancy with a much different outlook than the tests performed at Hospital 31 which had indicated that I had an abnormal pregnancy and the baby was destined to die. During my entire stay at this hospital I was under constant psychological pressure since the room where I was hospitalized was a double. A different woman was admitted to that room every day to subject her to an abortion (it is legal in Russia), and by noon she had left. Every day I tried to convince each one of those women that from the first moment of pregnancy there was a new life, a human being from the moment of conception and that to abort was a crime. I was only able to convince one young woman, and she left before the surgeon called her to perform the abortion; the doctor came later to admonish me and tell me that women entered the hospital voluntarily and that they could not let me make any propaganda against abortion (abortions are very expensive in this and other hospitals; they are abortion factories). Given the situation, my husband and I decided that I should leave as soon as possible.

Other difficulties arose during my pregnancy that we had to overcome, because the pressures for me to abort did not cease until I gave birth. It was through our faith in God, in the Holy Virgin Mary and our prayers to John Paul II to intercede for us before Providence that we have come through, and Marianna Letizia de Jesus was born (this is how she is baptized).                                    *Socorro (Russia)*

# 5 Floribeth, the Miracle that Made John Paul II a Saint

It all began on April 8, 2011 at six o'clock in the morning when upon waking up, Floribeth Mora Diaz, a forty-eight year old woman from Costa Rica, felt a terrible headache. Even though she already suffered from frequent headaches, this one in particular was unbearable. She grabbed her head with both hands. The pain would not diminish. Uncontrollable vomiting began. She did not understand what was happening to her. Very frightened, she asked Edwin, her husband, to take her to a hospital because she felt terrible. Two hours later, while at the Max Peralta Hospital in the city of Cartago, a doctor diagnosed that her severe migraines were due to excessive work and stress. Floribeth, a mother of four children, and at that moment grandmother of two grandchildren with another two on the way, worked full time and had returned to the university to study law.

She was given an injection and told to return home. Her husband decided to take her to a cabin in the woods, in Guanacaste, so that she could rest for a few days. "I took her to the cabin and we spent three days there. But my God," commented Edwin, at his Tres Rios' home on the outskirts of San José, Costa Rica, "I never imagined that I was carrying a time bomb, for she could have died at any moment."

Despite the rest, the headaches did not disappear. Upon returning to the city, they went to a pharmacy to have some medication prescribed for her. The doctor checked her blood pressure, noticed that it was very high, and told her to go to a hospital immediately. "My husband," Floribeth narrated, "took me to a friend of his who is a physician and has a private clinic. He examined me, made movements with my arms and legs, and upon checking the bottom of my eyes detected a stroke, a small drop of blood in the brain that was triggering the terrible pain. He immediately sent me to the hospital to be treated."

Floribeth went to the hospital's emergency room and was then admitted. A computerized axial tomography (CAT scan) was performed, which confirmed bleeding inside her brain. After an operation to attempt to repair the damage, the doctor told her that there was nothing they could do for her. He went on to explain that they needed to close the artery with an aluminum clip to stop the bleeding, but could not do it because the stroke had occurred in an inaccessible area of the brain.

The world came crashing down on Floribeth and Edwin. They understood that she could not be saved. Anguish overtook them. Floribeth wanted to see her mother, her sisters. She clung to her husband, and asked him not to let her die.

Jacqueline, one of Floribeth's sisters, shared in their suffering, hope, and prayers:

> During those days at the hospital, we were allowed
> to visit and talk to her, one at a time. I remember
> that in the little time I had with her we talked about
> the children, and her worry of not wanting to die.
> At that moment her main concern was her children,
> her husband, and grandchildren. One has no words

when someone tells you about not wanting to die, and you have no words because in reality only God decides. Sometimes I am afraid to contradict Him, that nothing will happen, because I don't know what God's will is. The only thing I could tell her was that we will pray to God for everything to turn out well. She was worried; we prayed, and that day I made the sign of the cross on her forehead; she wanted to see all of her children; we then retired because the rest of the family was back at the house waiting for news.

When Jacqueline arrived at her mother's house, she found her older brothers, who could not believe that Floribeth was so gravely ill. It was most surprising to observe Floribeth's mother, eighty-nine years old, and her attitude when the family tried to hide the reality of the situation from her.

I entered my mother's room and she was praying the rosary as always. I remember that I tried to explain Floribeth's health situation to her, but she interrupted me and said: "I am her mother; why is this being hidden from me if I am her mother? I need to be spoken to with clarity." I then told her what the doctor had explained to us, and that we needed to be prepared. That was my first gut feeling, to be prepared, one's logical side. I remember my mother telling me: "In my heart, I feel that this is not the case." This was a shock to me. I did not know whether to think that she did not want to accept reality, or that I lacked faith. I then left the room and went to talk with my brothers. We talked about how to support her children during these difficult times and agreed that we would go to their homes to support them while Flor was at the hospital with her husband.

Floribeth was interned at the hospital for seven days, receiving medication to help her with her pain and high blood pressure, while the doctors tried to figure out what they could do. As Holy Week approached, it was decided to release her from the hospital so that she could spend it with her family. They again explained to her that there was no possibility of performing surgery in Costa Rica, and even so it would have put her life at risk anyway.

> I was given one month to live. My husband was told that I would receive treatment during that period of time, which would keep me asleep to keep me calm and stable. I was always asleep as a result of the medication.

The doctors told Edwin that there was nothing else they could do for her, and that he had to take her home:

> I became very nervous and felt afraid. Tears trickled down my cheeks, but I did not want to cry in front of her because I had already cried so much. She stared at me and told me: "My love, don't let me die; I don't want to die." I told her: "No my love, I am going to help you." But inside me I thought: "How can I help her if I am caught in a circle from which I can't get out?" What could I do in this case?

Floribeth kept asking him not to let her die, and he continued to tell her that she would not die. "I told her, 'No my love, be calm, you are not going to die.' I consoled her, but I was broken up inside."

The doctor told Edwin that she could be operated on in either Mexico or Cuba, but one way or the other she would either die or end up in a vegetative state. When Edwin left the hospital, he felt the weight of the entire world on his shoulders. He started to cry, called his sons for them to reach their sister who lived in Mexico to see if she could help find a hospital where Floribeth could be operated on. What tormented him at that moment was that he realized that she had changed; she was tired and discouraged.

I saw a changed woman, an exhausted and desperate woman, how can I say it, like someone running from death. When I looked at her I wanted to cry, but did not do it in front of her and would tell her: "Be quiet my love, be calm, you are not going to die. I am going to do everything I can, if I have to sell everything and live on the street, I will live on the street, but you are not going to die on me."

I sat on a bench outside the hospital, lowered my head and cried for a while. I said: "My God, help me. Karol Wojtyla, John Paul II, don't leave me alone. Help me. I believe in you Holy Pope. John Paul II, you are a saint to me, help me, help me." And I recall, as if it were happening right now, hearing a voice that said: "Don't be afraid. Take her. Take her." He repeated "take her" twice: "Don't be afraid. Take her. Take her." I still remained there, thinking, crying, even with the faith that I have, but faith is lacking in one who still remained there, doubting. I stood up and thought: "He told me to take her, and I will take her."

Edwin had been part of John Paul II's security detail during his visit to Costa Rica twenty-nine years earlier. During that visit, he never imagined that he would ever reach out him, looking for a miracle.

Just before leaving the hospital, the doctor told him: "She can last one, two hours, a day, a month, perhaps longer, but she will die." They returned home where Floribeth had slept practically all day because of the medications she was taking. She had neither the strength nor any desire to do anything; she would start talking to one of her children, but would immediately fall asleep.

A few days later, while Floribeth slept from taking medication for her headaches which persisted, the family decided to make a small altar in the home, with an image of John Paul II, the baby Jesus and the Virgin of Fatima, of whom they are also devotees.

On April 30th she decided to go to Mass despite the pain she was feeling and the critical condition she was in, and from there she would go to the Temple of Our Lady of Pilar in the locality of Tres Rios where she lives.

"We waited for the Blessed Sacrament procession to pass, and I felt that something extraordinary was occurring." The priest carrying the Blessed Sacrament turned in our direction and gave us his blessing.

Then May 1st, the day of John Paul II's beatification, came. A prayer vigil had been organized at the San José Stadium. From there people could watch the live TV transmission from the Vatican. Floribeth's relatives, with Jacqueline among them, decided that they would go to the stadium to ask John Paul II for a miracle.

Jacqueline remembers:

We arrived there to pray, with contrite and sorrowful hearts. We arrived full of anguish and pain. There were so many things, so many questions that one asks when someone in the family is sick, so many questions; one does not want to go against God's will, but questions come up; I asked God, I asked the Pope to please intercede for all of our petitions, not only for my sister, but for all of us; that if He wanted to heal us, He would grant us healing, all for His glory and honor, not to glorify men or for fame, but for God's glory, for the world to know that even in this sad time, where sometimes there is no hope, He keeps granting miracles.

Jacqueline asked for John Paul II's intercession because for her he was a saint who had known suffering.

I said to myself: To me, John Paul II was not a saint because he was perfect. I saw him as a saint because in his humanity he taught us to endure suffering, pain and sickness. One would sometimes see his sick body but also notice his gaze on television, and that he had a very strong spirit.

Of course Floribeth could not go to the stadium. She made a decision to do her best not to fall asleep during the beatification ceremony. She recalled that thirty years ago she was one of the young people who had received John Paul II with overwhelming enthusiasm at the National Stadium, where the Pope had asked them to say "No to selfishness, no to injustice, no to despair, no to hatred, no to ways without God," but to say instead "Yes to faith, yes to justice, yes to love, yes to peace, yes to solidarity, especially with the needy, and yes to hope."

I asked God to not let me fall asleep because I wanted to watch the transmission. I fell asleep, but thanks be to God I was able to wake up at 2:30 in the morning because it would be 3:00 in the morning in Costa Rica during the Vatican transmission. I was able watch the Mass, always asking the Lord to help me because I did not want to die; I wanted to be with my children; I wanted to live to get to know the two grandsons who were on their way. I did not want to leave my youngest son, who worried me the most.

After she finished watching the ceremony, she fell asleep. The next morning she woke up around 8:00 in the morning.

When I woke up the next day, my husband was already in the kitchen. I was reading a magazine that had a picture of John Paul II on its front page. I crossed myself as I do every day, giving thanks to the Lord for a new day; I continued to read the magazine about John Paul, admiring him, observing him, and listening to his voice which said: "Get up. Don't be afraid." I saw his hands gesturing towards me, inviting me to get up. I was amazed, kept looking at the magazine and told him: "Yes my Lord." That was my answer.

Floribeth got out of bed and went to the kitchen where her husband was preparing breakfast. Edwin could not believe what he was seeing. He asked her what she was doing up. Floribeth responded that she felt fine, but did not tell him what had happened. "I was afraid to tell him about what was happening at that moment because they would believe I was crazy. After all, I am taking medication to keep me asleep; who is going to believe me? They will say it is a reaction to the medication."

As the hours went by, Floribeth continued to feel well. Little by little, she told Edwin what had happened to her. He recalled what had happened to him outside the hospital. They both understood that John Paul II had granted them the miracle of her healing. They began to tell their children and relatives.

Two months later they learned that a relic of John Paul II had arrived at Cartago from Poland. They decided to go to the Paraiso Parish but got there late, when their doors were already closed. They approached nonetheless. A security guard told them to return the next day, but Providence had other plans.

Father Donald, the church's pastor, saw them from afar and approached them to ask them what they wanted. After listening to them, and without knowing why, he decided to let them in to show them the relic, an ampoule with a few drops of John Paul II's blood in it. This would turn out to be providential for the Vatican to find her, after reading her testimony which she sent to the Postulator's Office months later to support the cause of John Paul II's canonization.

Father Donald recalled: "I took them to the House of the Curia, and honestly, at that moment I was afraid to open the doors to the house to two strangers because I did not know them. It was then that I told them to wait for me on the terrace. I took the relic to them there, where they had their first encounter." The first thing that Father Donald did was to give the relic to Floribeth. She crossed herself, embraced it, embraced her husband and then they told Father Donald that they were certain that John Paul II had granted them a miracle.

Father Donald explained to them that the ampoule with John Paul II's blood in it had been brought by a Polish priest friend of his. It turns out that it was Father Dariusz, secretary of Cardinal Stanislaw Dziwisz, who was John Paul II's secretary for forty years. Floribeth and Edwin tried to see him but he was resting. Through Father Donald, they sent him a small holy card with John Paul II's image and with a phrase written in Polish: "Do not be afraid."

The next day Floribeth and her husband took a flower arrangement to Father Donald for the altar he was making for the relic.

Six months after suffering the stroke, Floribeth was subjected to follow-up exams:

"I was very calm, very calm," Floribeth remembers. "I was not afraid, but had a lot of faith in what was to be. When the doctor saw the resonance, he was surprised at not seeing any signs of the aneurism. It was not there." The doctor did not give any credit. "It's just that there is nothing there," he told them. It was at that moment that they realized that they were truly dealing with a miraculous healing.

"We left the hospital very excited. I, most grateful to the Lord, for because of the faith I had, I knew I didn't have anything; I had that conviction." Months later they did another resonance exam. While she was in the machine, the doctor asked her who had diagnosed her with an aneurism. There was neither a trace nor any ill effects from it. "I have no ill effects of any kind, from the cerebral event that occurred. Supposedly," Floribeth explained, "the left side of my body should be paralyzed, but it is not; I never lost consciousness, my eyesight, or movement in any of my extremities; I walk perfectly, continue my studies, and keep on living normally since May 1st when he told me to get up, until this day."

Doctor Juan Antonio Valverde Espinosa, a neurology and internal medicine specialist at Dr. Max Peralta de Cartago Hospital, performed the evaluation of Floribeth's clinical profile, which is found among the records sent to the Vatican.

During the investigation process, the doctor declared not knowing of any significant study or report about the spontaneous disappearance of fusiform aneurisms without surgical procedures being performed. "There are no scientific elements," he stated, "that help explain an aneurism's disappearance." According to the specialist, the disappearance of "an aneurysmal arterial injury is a phenomenon which transcends any medically demonstrable explanation through existing analysis."

Neurosurgeon Alejandro Vargas Roman, who cared for Floribeth at the Calderon Guardia Hospital and discovered that she had suffered a stroke, had no answers to the fusiform aneurism's disappearance, because the stroke had to do with the expansion of the entire circumference of the artery causing bleeding in the brain.

Floribeth's case was even examined by means of a Latin-American symposium that took place in Mexico, where the doctors agreed in that it could not be operated on, but only treated with conservative means that might still not have saved her life.

Doctor Alejandro Vargas Roman is Catholic and his experience as a doctor has made him think that miracles do exist, but he discards the idea that his beliefs could have clouded his judgment. "All exams that were performed, both here as well as at Gemelli Hospital in Rome, demonstrated that the aneurism disappeared without a medical explanation."

Because of this inexplicable healing from a scientific point of view, Edwin encouraged Floribeth to write her testimony and send it to the Vatican so that the world could learn about the marvelous things that John Paul II does. Floribeth found an Internet website with many testimonies of miracles received, and wrote her own.

"I wanted the world to realize that God had performed a miracle in me, and what a better way to tell the world than through the Internet." Fortunately, Floribeth mentioned both Father Donald and Father Dariusz, the Polish priest who had brought John Paul II's relic to Costa Rica, in her story. "Thanks to that," Father Donald explained, "we could find Floribeth, and the official process began." In fact, shortly thereafter the Postulator's Office got in touch with her and asked her to send all the medical exams to which she had been subjected since the stroke was diagnosed to the Vatican. Floribeth recalled:

> I cried because I said to myself: "My God, of all the testimonies on this web page, they have turned their gaze towards this miserable, insignificant woman in God's eyes, from a distant town, San Jose, and such a small country like Costa Rica." I felt so honored that they were interested in me.

Meanwhile at the Vatican, Maria Victoria Hernandez, a Spaniard who since the first day worked at the Postulator's Office for the cause of John Paul II's beatification, and now canonization, had the task of reading Floribeth's testimony. During this process, and due to the large number of letters and e-mails from that region with cases regarding graces or supposed miracles received as a result of John Paul II's intercessions, she had to make a long virtual voyage throughout Latin America. She narrated:

Throughout all these years, I was impressed with Costa Rica because of its devotion to John Paul II, its unity, its young people's participation in the initiatives organized by the ecclesiastic hierarchy to celebrate the beatification. Above all, I was moved by the faith of the "tico" people. I was convinced that the miracle to fulfill the canonization had to come from Latin America, and thought that it would be marvelous if John Paul II had performed it exactly on the day of his beatification. And that's how it happened.

After the beatification, the office received a torrent of testimonies. Among all of those, a few were selected that had been subjected to previous examination. On February 23, 2012, and during a break, Maria Victoria checked the e-mails both in Spanish and Portuguese, just as she had for the cause in 2005.

Floribeth's was among the first messages I read, followed by another coming from Mexico City. The one from Mexico was the case of Santiago, fifteen months old, healed from a very serious heart condition, an *aortic stenosis* in three sectors.

I recall that Floribeth's got my attention because it had to do with an aneurism, something I knew that could be fatal, that it had not been possible to intervene surgically, and that healing was immediate and total. Additionally, it came from Costa Rica, and had occurred on the same day as the beatification. Certainly I could not ask for more.

Months earlier they had started to examine the supposedly miraculous healing of a Lebanese girl, but the case did not proceed. It was then decided to examine Floribeth's case. She was always certain, as she insistently communicated in the messages she exchanged with Maria Victoria, that it had been a grace that was not just for her but for the Glory of God.

On many occasions Floribeth wrote to her to thank her for having read her testimony and to have sensed somehow that this could be the one that led to John Paul II's canonization. On one occasion she wrote:

> It is really a miracle because of my Holy Father John Paul II's intercession. Imagine, after such a near-fatal incident I have been a surprise for the doctors, because my physical and mental faculties are in excellent shape. Everything is for God's glory and honor. I take this opportunity to tell you that I am thankful that you read my testimony, and must tell everyone that he is a saint to us.

The months following the beatification were marked by a personal event that could have had very serious consequences for Maria Victoria.

"Just as I translated the two testimonies, the one from the Lebanese girl and Floribeth's, I discovered a cyst that turned out to be a malignant tumor." Maria prayed to God's servant, Tomas Morales Perez, of whom she is the postulator for his beatification, and Blessed John Paul II.

> Providence wanted the bonds with John Paul II to become even stronger. This is how the same doctor who examined the case of the Lebanese girl, took care of mine, putting me in the hands of doctors with great human and professional competence.

To Maria Victoria, there is no doubt that Blessed John Paul II was behind what could have been a fatal ending for her.

They detected the malignant tumor in due time, and somehow this circumstance indissolubly sealed the friendship that she had reestablished with John Paul II all these years since the day after May 13, 2005 when Pope Benedict XVI granted the dispensation to begin the cause for his beatification.

What is extraordinary in the causes of beatification and canonization, is that God speaks in different languages. From the beginning of the cause for John Paul II, a large volume of electronic mail and letters was received, as well as messages that were left on the Polish Pope's tomb.

What is interesting is that in the case of both beatification and canonization, the protagonists of the miracles that made it possible for John Paul II to be beatified and later canonized were two women, and in both cases these miracles were discovered by women.

In the case of Sister Marie Simon-Pierre's inexplicable healing, when she was afflicted with Parkinson's disease and became healed exactly two months after John Paul II's death, the intuition of Michele Smits who, like Maria Victoria worked in the Postulator's Office from the beginning, was determinant. Because she is French, she was tasked with reading the testimony of Marie Simon-Pierre's Superior. In both situations, the common denominator that immediately attracted their attention was the simplicity with which they told about the event, and the humility of the people in these *grace tsunamis*, who at no time displayed any kind of desire to call attention to themselves.

In the case of Sister Marie Simon-Pierre, they thanked God for making possible that the sister who worked in a maternity hospital could continue to dedicate herself to the care of newborns. In fact, when she was informed that all the sisters in her congregation were going to pray a "novena" asking for John Paul II's intercession, she limited herself to say that she submitted to God's will and, whether it be in sickness or through healing, she only wanted it to be for God's glory and the congregation's spiritual well-being.

In Floribeth's case, the sudden aneurism almost ended the life of a wife, mother and grandmother. Floribeth did not pray for herself; she prayed to John Paul II because she did not want to leave her children and grandchildren. In both miracles, John Paul II demonstrated himself as the saint of families, of life, and protector of the same.

Unfortunately the exams that Floribeth sent to the Vatican after it was decided to examine her case, did not clarify all the doubts that the Italian doctors consulted by the Postulator's Office still had. Floribeth was asked to travel to Rome to be subjected to new and even more sophisticated controls at the Gemelli Hospital, which John Paul II called "Vatican Number Three" for the many days he spent there.

Despite knowing that the exams she would have to undergo were complicated, painful and even risky, Floribeth and her husband agreed to travel to Italy.

"In the Vatican, I felt like a peasant arriving in a big city. To be in Rome was an honor and a privilege that God granted me," she confessed as she recalled her trip to the Italian capital to undergo medical exams as part of the investigation.

She was hospitalized for one week. They performed all the required exams. Upon exiting the hospital she began to feel ill.

She vomited all day, and had a high fever. Her stay coincided with October 22, the day of the Feast of the Blessed John Paul II. A Mass was celebrated in front of his tomb in the St. Sebastian Chapel, next to Michelangelo's Pietà in St. Peter's Basilica. Floribeth attended but was not feeling very well. Upon returning home she learned that she had been infected by a virus.

To be in front of John Paul II's tomb triggered very strong emotions for both her and her husband. "When we were standing at John Paul II's tomb," they recalled, "it was like a dream; we could not believe it. We felt chills, a very strong emotion, the urge to cry, because we never imagined being able get to where he is."

After the Italian doctors analyzed the results from all the exams, they confirmed that in their opinion this was about an inexplicable healing from a scientific point of view. The diocesan process to canonize John Paul II could now begin.

I contacted the archbishopric of San Jose, Costa Rica and asked to be seen by the Archbishop, who at that time was Monsignor Hugo Barrantes. He could not hide his great satisfaction at receiving such news. "It is exciting," he commented when he learned about it, "that despite being such a small country, God has chosen us through John Paul II to grant a miracle and go down in history." Additionally, he had a theory as to why Costa Rica had been chosen. In his opinion, it was because of the great treatment John Paul II received when he visited the country in 1993, and also because he did not want Costa Rica to become a secularist country. It was a great surprise for what Costa Rica represents, in reality a small country in the middle of the universal Church. "It is a gift from God, a gift from John Paul II to us," the Archbishop explained, "because it means that in a country that walks in giant steps towards secularization, there is still faith, there is still belief in our Lord Jesus Christ, and that the Church continues to be present. Then, in reality, it has been strength, a push, an injection of faith in the middle of so many situations, sometimes complicated, that the Church can find herself in here."

I traveled to Costa Rica on two occasions. The second was to open the diocesan process. It lasted from November 20 until December 2. We listened to eleven witnesses. *Monsignor Slawomir Oder*

Floribeth and Edwin are certain that John Paul II granted them two miracles. In addition to Floribeth's healing, the miracle had an extraordinary impact on the reinforcement of the family's faith and unity. "The second miracle," Floribeth told us with tears in her eyes, "was that my husband realized how important I was to him." In the midst of suffering and anguish, even the couple's four children became more united as a family, and those who had withdrawn from the Church rediscovered their faith.

Their family life was not without tribulations and difficult moments. Fifteen years ago, the child who would have been their fourth son was born dead. Supposedly after this loss she should not have been able to have any more children, but after two years Floribeth became pregnant with Keyner, who was born after her sixth month of pregnancy; he is now fourteen years of age and was her main concern during her illness.

Since Floribeth was healed, John Paul II made her feel his

presence at various moments. Her daughter Monica could not get pregnant. When Floribeth and Edwin traveled to Rome to undergo the controls at the Gemelli Hospital, they went to John Paul II's tomb and took a special petition with them where they asked that their daughter be able to have children. The Pope listened to their prayer.

During Floribeth's illness, her daughter Gabriela, twenty-six years old, realized that she was pregnant with her first child. She needed her mother more than ever because they were always very close, but she also had to care for her mother, while at the same time worry about her pregnancy. She was hardly ever told anything about her mother's condition in fear of affecting her, but that increased her anguish. Even though she wasn't the oldest sibling, she provided support to her brothers. After her mother's healing she once again became pregnant and made a decision: her daughter would be named Victoria. She was tempted to name her Milagro, but finally decided to keep the first name because of her mother's victory over death.

Before his mother's illness, Edwin, her twenty-five year old son, had distanced himself from the Church. What he lived through, changed his life:

> I cannot forget the day I entered the hospital and saw my mother in critical condition. She gave us her blessing. She said goodbye to us. We cried "enough": we did not want to leave the hospital and were almost thrown out because we did not want to leave her bedside. She bid us goodbye and told me: "Edwin, I love you very much, take care of your family, and your sisters." It was very hard. I left that hospital in a shambles, took my daughters and cried with them;

I embraced my father. He cried, and was somebody completely different because he was totally lost.

Young Edwin prayed to Pope John Paul II to say "enough," to the point of even telling him that he would give his life in return for his mother to be kept alive. "I told the Pope that I would exchange my life for hers. Neither my brothers nor I felt prepared to lose her."

Now they don't know how to thank God and John Paul II enough that their mother is alive. "We give thanks to God, to Jesus Christ, to John Paul II, but do not find how to act for the good; we want to find a way to return the favor by behaving well."

# 6 John Paul II's Relics

During his twenty-six year pontificate, John Paul II covered the distance between the Earth and the Moon three times. In his one hundred and four trips he traveled one million, two hundred thousand kilometers (some 750,000 miles), which represents going around the world twenty-nine times.

One day we asked him why he traveled so much. He responded: "Because I am Peter's successor, but also Paul's, the great missionary."

He felt the need to deliver Christ's message, which to him was above all a message of peace, throughout the world, even to the most remote and forgotten places on earth.

He accompanied peoples and nations in their good, but also painful moments. He advocated tirelessly for conflicts to cease, was a peace negotiator, and traveled to bastions of terrorists and extremists.

Three million people poured into Rome to bid him goodbye during his last days. They arrived to accompany him during the last phase of his earthly pilgrimage, because he had accompanied them, during the good and the bad, for more than a quarter of a century. He had kissed the soil of their lands, a gesture laden with their joys, sufferings, disappointments, and hopes. A profound nostalgia spread all over the world after his death. A planetary nostalgia set in, accompanied by a strong feeling of being orphaned.

Countries afflicted by violence and conflict felt the need of his presence, his words of peace and hope. Out of this need, this nostalgia, the idea of a traveling relic emerged.

The presence of a relic cannot be understood as a "magical" presence. The relic has meaning only if it refers to the person it represents; the message and meaning of his life and, in John Paul II's case, his teaching.

To all the places that John Paul II's relic was taken, it was clear that the message of love that the Pope sowed remains alive among people. His love of Christ was the starting point of his love for all human beings; his deep affection for human beings touched the hearts of men and women, regardless of their race, color, religion or social level.

Devotion to his relic on the part of millions of people around the world was the answer to what he had sowed in life. His generous service to humanity, marked by his love for evangelizing, has not been forgotten in any locale as is clear from looking at a map that highlights all the places that a relic of John Paul II has visited. The number of places on all continents where a relic was sent so that it could remain permanently in a church, convent or seminary, is impressive.

A relic even reached countries to which John Paul II could not travel. One was even sent to Kamchatka, in Eastern Russia; another to Lebanon, Mongolia, Kazakhstan, Japan, India, Shanghai, Hong Kong, and Vietnam as well as the Philippines, Guam, Australia, and New Zealand.

In the African continent one is also found in Benin, Nigeria, Zambia, Rwanda and Tanzania. Many European and American countries have also asked to have a relic.

Over the last several years, and as a gesture of gratitude for having received a relic, many moving testimonies to the cause of his canonization have arrived at the Postulator's Office.

A priest from a small Italian parish was moved to see many young people, who had distanced themselves from the Church, return during the week that the relic was there.

In Our Lady of Egypt Parish in Montreal, Canada, on the last evening the relic would be present, and after a grueling week of activities related to Blessed John Paul II in which many of the faithful participated, three young people with multiple tattoos and piercings entered the church. It was close to midnight when Don Emir, the Egyptian community's pastor, was about to close the church's doors. The three youths told the priest that they had become aware through their friends that there was something unusual there, and did not understand what it was about. The pastor explained to them that it was John Paul II's blood. The three youths became perplexed, started to pray and after a few minutes, asked to be confessed. It was their first confession in many years.

A young pastor from St. Augustine Church, in Kendall Park, New Jersey, USA, witnessed the healing of one of his collaborators afflicted with leukemia, after the relic's stay in his church. In appreciation for this healing, many faithful began to arrive to the parish, even from adjacent states.

A young Canadian named Ana from Quebec told us that in 1984, when John Paul II visited Canada for the first time and traveled from Quebec to Montreal by train, she was going through a very difficult moment in her life, marked by rebellion, family problems and several complicated relationships.

Ana's house was very near Quebec's train station. She became curious and opened the window to see the Pope. At that very moment, the wagon in which John Paul II was traveling and greeting people through its small window passed by. It was only for a single moment, but their gazes crossed. The Pope smiled to her and gave her his blessing. To her, that gaze and smile represented the beginning of a conversion that changed her life. She said that from that moment, she felt loved, and her life acquired a new meaning.

Ana had mailed her testimony to the Postulator's Office at the beginning of John Paul II's beatification process. When she learned that the relic was about to arrive in Quebec, she decided to go and venerate it because many years before, the Pope had restored hope in her and the desire to live.

One special fruit of the relic's presence was harvested in Talavera de la Reina in Spain, where a conference about the relationship between John Paul II and Carmel took place. It was a very spiritual and intense experience.

John Paul always wore a scapular, having been attracted to the Carmelite spirituality since his youth when he used to visit the Carmelite parish in his hometown of Wadowice. His spiritual guide, Jan Tyranowski, had him knock on the door of Cracow's Carmelite Fathers' monastery, which he wanted to enter to become a monk. God has disposed otherwise. As a result of the Nazi invasion, the monastery could not receive new candidates, and Karol's vocation changed course towards the diocesan seminary, which he entered clandestinely.

In Talavera de la Reina, it was impressive to see young people participate in the life of the nuns' monastery. In spite of the cloister, there was friendship and communion among them. There was great participation both in the conference and the veneration of John Paul II's relic. Months later, a letter from the Carmelite nuns arrived at the Postulator's Office to inform them that after their encounter with the relic, three young women entered the convent. One of them had been singled out by John Paul II in Rome when she participated on the Palm Sunday when he initiated the World Youth Jubilee in 1984. The other two had felt the call during the veneration of the relic. The youngest of them had not yet turned eighteen years of age and resisted the calling. She always came up with excuses; her age, the university, her family's wishes, until she came in contact with John Paul II's relic. The young woman wrote to the Postulator's office:

> During the adoration vigil, I tried to hold back tears to avoid calling attention to myself; I found it exciting to think that I was at the place where God wanted me to spend my life committed to Him and where, in John Paul II's presence, I felt full of grace. It seemed as if he were there among us and he was giving me the push I needed to overcome the fear that was holding me back. I felt especially excited when Eloy the seminarian, and now Deacon, who was there suggested to me that I take the relic up to the main door, and hand it over to the Mother Superior to be venerated during the closing evening.
>
> I will never forget the moment when I was carrying John Paul II's own blood in my hands, to see the convent's main door open, and the entire community waiting inside. I can assure you that I did not lack desire to sneak into the cloister, and remain there forever. I cried like a baby at that moment, it was impossible to contain myself. I then started my studies at the university knowing that the following year, when I would be old enough, I too could cross the convent's main door that the relic had crossed.

A letter reached the Postulator's Office from a Vietnamese woman, a country from which news is always arriving about the difficulties and heroic fidelity that Catholics face in trying to live their faith. The woman was asking for a relic to be sent to her to be placed in her home's oratory. According to the norms of the Congregation for Divine Worship, a relic cannot be sent to an individual home, only to a church, seminary, or monastery. Due to the woman's insistence, the relic was sent to her Bishop. It was later learned that the woman's house had become a type of *domus ecclesiae*, similar to the beginning of Christianity in the West. For months, the oratory was the object of pilgrimages from the faithful who came there from different provinces. Recently, a church was built and John Paul II's relic was transferred there. A picture of John Paul II was placed next to the altar. His relic seems to give strength to Christians persecuted not only in Vietnam but in other countries as well, such as China and North Korea.

The case of the Auxiliary Bishop of Saigon, François Xavier Nguyen Van Thuan, jailed for thirteen years and made Cardinal by John Paul II after his liberation, remains a bright example. Providence wanted John Paul II's canonization to coincide with the closing of the diocesan process for the cause of the beatification of this persecution martyr in Vietnam.

John Paul II's relic reached Hong Kong. John Paul II's wish to travel to China, even though in symbolic fashion, became a reality through his relic, six years after his death.

It was a very emotional moment when the Postulator's Office received a letter in which the Bishop of Hong Kong asked for a relic. The response was immediate. With the Vatican's Secretary of State's help, a lock of the Blessed's hair was sent immediately. The Vicar General of the Diocese was surprised by the prompt response. "Maybe," he commented, "it was because we are a Chinese Diocese."

To somehow have been able to realize the Pope's dream of traveling to China was one of the Postulator's Office's most significant moments after John Paul II's beatification. There is hope that the relic's presence in Hong Kong represents the beginning of a new springtime for the Chinese Catholic Church. It would be another miracle by the now saint.

There is a place in the world that, within the framework of John Paul II's canonization, has a significant and symbolic meaning. The Nuestra Señora del Rescate de Ujarrás Parish, in Paraiso, Cartago Province, a few kilometers from San José, Costa Rica is where the relic, a drop of blood inside a reliquary, arrived on July 2, 2011; this was exactly two years before the Congregation for the Causes of Saints approved the miraculous healing of Floribeth Mora Diaz, who by the design of Providence was in contact with the relic.

Father Donald Solano (who in his years of study in Italy, had providentially known the Polish priest Dariusz Ras, who would become Cardinal Stanislaw Dziwisz's secretary, who in turn had been John Paul II's secretary for forty years) led the initiative. They had remained in contact, and Father Donald had invited Father Dariusz to visit him in Costa Rica. Once the details of the trip could be finalized, Father Donald asked Father Dariusz to bring a relic of John Paul II for his parish. Had this not occurred, it would have been almost impossible to find Floribeth since the testimony of her healing did not include any specifics about her. The only concrete element that led to her whereabouts was the story of her visit to the Paraiso de Cartago parish, and having mentioned Father Donald and Father Dariusz.

Additionally, Father Donald's church is given credit for

having allowed Floribeth and her husband to enter the church after it had closed for the evening and it was no longer possible to see the relic.

There is no doubt that the relic's presence in Cartago had a providential role in the positive outcome of John Paul II's canonization. It had been thirty years since Father Donald, forty-five years old, was one of the many youths who participated in the encounter with John Paul II at San José's National Stadium.

That encounter marked him profoundly. Years later he entered the seminary and went to study in Rome where he talked to the Pope on three occasions.

He decided to ask Father Dariusz for a relic to get his faithful close to a saintly man, to make them understand that a spiritual friendship can be established with people who have been saints in life, and ask for their intercession, even though the miracles come from God and not the relic itself.

Thousands of people have prayed before the relic since it first arrived at his parish, many of them in search of a physical or spiritual cure. To this day he can't explain why he made the decision to allow Floribeth and her husband, people whom he did not know because they were not part of his congregation, to come in.

Father Donald was one of the first people whom the couple told about John Paul II's having granted a miracle to Floribeth. At that moment he never imagined that he would be tasked with finding them after their testimony was read at the Postulator's Office, and accompany them to Rome when Floribeth had to undergo new exams at the Gemelli Hospital. He never imagined that God would use him as a providential instrument in the canonization process.

One of his most emotional memories is to have seen Floribeth and her husband pray before John Paul II's tomb, to have been able to kneel with them and give thanks for Floribeth's healing. They participated in a Mass to celebrate October 22, the Blessed's feast, in front of his tomb. There were about three hundred people in attendance, but only they knew why they were there.

## Mexico

On May 1, 2011, the day of John Paul II's beatification, millions of Mexicans saw Mother Tobiana (the Polish religious sister who had been John Paul II's shadow, especially during the last years of his life), next to Sister Marie Simon-Pierre (who had been miraculously cured from Parkinson's), walk up to Pope Benedict XVI and leave a relic from the Blessed Pope on a pedestal. It was an ampoule with drops of his blood extracted during the last days of his life. In that relic, they saw an extension of what John Paul II had meant to them and Mexico.

Because of the situation of violence and insecurity that the country was living through, a spontaneous faithful movement emerged asking their priests and bishops to bring a relic from the "Mexican Pope" as a symbol of hope and reconciliation.

Father Manuel Corral Martin, the spokesperson for the Mexican Episcopal Conference, and Antonio Berumen who participated in the organization of all of John Paul II's visits to Mexico, understood the people's anguish and what it would mean to them to have John Paul II back in their midst again.

The Mexican Episcopal Conference unanimously approved the touring of the Blessed's relic; it was decided that John Paul II's relic would visit all ninety-one dioceses, something he was not able to do in life.

On several occasions and upon returning from a trip to Mexico, John Paul II commented that in order to tend to all invitations from the Mexican Bishops, he would have had to remain in Mexico for three months, something that would not have bothered him one bit but, he said laughing, he would not be allowed to.

To have given John Paul II's relic to Mexico as part of the postulation for the cause of his canonization, represented an act of justice, not only because Mexico had been the first country that John Paul II visited, but also because of the great love, totally requited by all Mexicans, that he felt for Mexico.

The Mexican Episcopate explained the pilgrimage's meaning:

> Plunged into terror, pain, hopelessness and rancor, consequences of the insecurity and violence perpetrated by those who have been inclined towards a culture of death, the relic's veneration will be an opportunity for the baptized and people of goodwill to turn their eyes back to God and, by John Paul II's intercession, obtain His forgiveness and mercy.

An elaborate wax statue with John Paul II's face and a reliquary in which an ampoule of his blood would be placed was ordered.

Thus an extraordinary 22,500 kilometer voyage began, and its theme was: "I remain with you at heart, and my love lives among all of you."

Beyond those critics who considered it a macabre manifestation of idolatry and magic, the pilgrimage revealed what John Paul II had meant to the lives of millions of Mexicans and the faith they continue to have in him. By standing in long lines to approach the catafalque and the relic, people felt that somehow John Paul II saw them from Heaven and prayed for them. During three months, and throughout the entire country, people stood in line for hours, day and night, singing, praying, chanting, cheering, as if John Paul II was still alive. That is how people, priests, bishops and cardinals in the diverse dioceses felt.

That caravan of hope and peace reached the most conflicted areas of the country.

Before the tour began, the Mexican bishops directed an appeal to all organized crime groups to allow the faithful to venerate the relic in peace, order and harmony. The response was immediate. People could be at ease that they and the relic would not be in any danger.

In fact, no violence erupted as the caravan, always under escort by Federal and State Police, moved through the more violent areas. Children, young people, adults, the elderly, the sick, armed gunmen and, it is said, even mafia bosses, prayed before the relic.

The people who for four months traveled with the relic could feel people's anguish and hopelessness, but at the same time, their desire to believe again, to have faith, to look to the future with greater serenity. Upon touching the glass that protected the catafalque, they somehow released their pain. When they arrived in a town, four people would effortlessly dismount the catafalque from the truck that was carrying it. Upon trying to retrieve it from the place where thousands of people had been touching it crying, screaming, praying for Mexico more than for themselves, they could not pick it up. They had to ask for help, as if it carried all the energy that people had deposited on it.

The most dramatic scenes were experienced in Ciudad Juarez, where the mothers of women who had disappeared, without being able to stop weeping, cried out their plights to John Paul to bring their daughters back, and not to abandon them. In ghost towns, where people no longer ventured outside their homes, thousands of people by day and by night invaded the streets to see the caravan go by; they even went onto the highways. In San Fernando, Tamaulipas, where a mass grave with one hundred and fifty-two mutilated bodies was discovered, people turned out crying, trying to tip the truck that carried the catafalque. The people were desperate, praying for those missing, embracing those in charge of the tour, asking them not to leave, to stay with them to give them strength. People perceived John Paul II's spiritual proximity, and to be able to approach the relic meant comfort to them.

The relic's impact on the sick was very well-known. As when he was alive, people with health problems approached the catafalque, and touched the glass with great faith. Mothers of sick children waited for hours to be able to walk near the wax statue and pray to John Paul for their children's health, as if he could hear them. Several cases similar to exorcisms were registered as well, as if the relic's presence could ward off evil. Newspapers captured the testimony of people on crutches or in wheelchairs, whose only wish was, for just one instant, to touch the glass that protected the wax statue, to give thanks for a miracle or invoke another. Reporters were told "faith can move mountains and that's why we are here." People commented that "John Paul II was very handsome and would help them get well." This was the case of Mrs. Rosario Rosa Garcia, who arrived with her one hundred and one year old mother who had been hospitalized with pneumonia for fifteen days and had been released despite a totally negative prognosis. According to Rosario, this happened because two weeks prior to the relic's arrival, she had entrusted herself to "John Paul II, the Virgin of Guadalupe, and God."

John Paul II's relic passed through all the places that the Pope had been in his five visits, along with others that he could not visit. It seemed that time stood still, and that thirty-two years had not passed. Inside and outside of the churches, one only heard boasts and cheers: "We see, we feel, the Pope is here among us!" "John Paul, our friend, the people are with you!" "John Paul, our brother, you are already a Mexican!" His presence in the Basilica of Our Lady of Guadalupe, where John Paul II knelt for the first time in January 1979 to place his present, future, joys and sufferings in the Morenita's hands, was particularly emotional. The same happened in Mexico's Cathedral, where he had asked all Mexicans to "always be faithful."

In giving the welcome at both churches, Cardinal Norberto Rivera Carrera, Archbishop of Mexico City, affirmed that the faith explosion that accompanied his five visits and that were demonstrated in the cheers "John Paul II, everyone loves you," or "John Paul, our brother, you are already a Mexican," remained alive six years after his death.

He also affirmed that the Mexicans' cheers forever remained in the Pope's soul, awakening "the conscience of his vocation as a peace pilgrim, like the voice of a Church that is light for the peoples and a reason for hope in the midst of adversity."

The Cardinal prayed to the Virgin of Guadalupe, through Blessed John Paul II's intercession, for the gift of peace and justice for Mexico.

I was so moved by the images of the pilgrimage that reached the Vatican that I myself decided to carry the relic through one of its pilgrimage stages. My turn came in Merida, Yucatan. I was seated in the truck that carried the relic. From there I could see how, still many kilometers away from the city, people had amassed along the road. I saw the truck inundated with flower petals; I saw people's hands coming close to the glass; mothers who seemed to hand their children over for me to touch them; I could feel the Mexican people's authentic faith when I realized their enormous love for John Paul II, which remained alive in their hearts and memory.

During Mass in Merida's Cathedral, celebrated by the city's Archbishop Monsignor Emilio Berlie, I saw how people prayed to thank God for having a great intercessor in Heaven.

In that church I was witness to the emotions of fifteen year old Estefania Guadalupe Ceballos Martin, who wanted to celebrate her fifteenth birthday with her entire family there, next to John Paul II's image. Rosy Polanco Ucan, who after waiting in line for five hours, also approached me to tell me that the day John Paul II arrived in Merida in 1993, she was admitted to the emergency room with a case of pneumonia. She was on the verge of death, but her family entrusted her to the Pope and she survived. "I came to thank him," she said.

I was also impressed with the ecclesial dimension of the strong relationship that the Mexicans have with the Pope. I had not observed it in any other country.

*Monsignor Slawomir Oder*

After a pilgrimage of one hundred and thirteen days, ninety-one dioceses, and at least one hundred localities, that ended in Cuernavaca, Morelos, Father Manuel Corral, responsible for the visit's organization, affirmed that the objective of praying for peace had been fully met. "The relic's presence brought hope to the Mexican people."

During an encounter with the country's bishops, Monsignor Christophe Pierre, nuncio in Mexico, recognized that this was an event that had astonished them and far exceeded their expectations. It showed that John Paul II "attracted each and every one toward heaven," that the multitudes that approached the relic everywhere, "fascinated by his sanctity," were impressive.

The relic's pilgrimage ended towards mid-December. As in every year, I traveled to Mexico with my family to vacation for a few days. I received a telephone call from Antonio Berumen, the pilgrimage's soul, who proposed to me that I be the person to return the relic to Rome. To my obvious surprise, and with great warmth, he said to me: "Who better than you?"

On January 5, 2011, at 5 o'clock in the afternoon, I arrived at Mexico City's Airport with my daughters, Rosario, my father's widow, her niece and several friends who had vacationed with us in Mexico. Father Manuel Corral was waiting for me in a room where he handed me a letter with which the Mexican Episcopate authorized me to leave the country with the relic. He had also brought me a blue backpack from the Episcopal Conference to put the relic's case in. I put it on like a shoulder bag "so I would not lose it!"

Everything went so fast. We bade farewell to each

other and, accompanied by airport personnel, I went to the boarding gate. Obviously I had to through a security checkpoint. I would have liked to have a camera to photograph the people that asked me: "What are you carrying there?" "John Paul II's relic," I answered. They looked at me as if looking at a space alien. The people who accompanied me confirmed the information. "The relic must pass through the metal detector," they told me. "Don't worry; it will be fine." I took off the backpack and placed on the belt. I did everything in slow and careful movements, as if I was handling a newborn baby. I felt a great responsibility and fear of not being able to fulfill the mission with which I had been entrusted.

Once I reached the airplane I behaved the same way. I didn't know whether to put the backpack in the upper compartment above my seat or simply leave it on. I opted for the latter.

Once the plane took off I began to relax. I remembered what had transpired during the flight to Mexico and thought that I should inform the crew. The stewardesses, all excited, told the captain immediately, who allowed me to enter the cabin with the relic. Both the pilot and co-pilot were Catholics and devotees of John Paul II. In a quiet moment during the flight, the captain brought all stewardesses together so that they could pray before the relic. I had also asked Father Manuel that if, in the event I was asked, the relic could be passed among the passengers. Since he had said, Yes, I made the proposal to the captain. Like his colleague on the flight from Madrid to Mexico did, the captain, through the cabin's loudspeakers, informed the passengers that they were carrying a very special passenger, John Paul II's relic. The passengers' reaction, especially the Spaniards and the Mexicans, was one of surprise and excitement at the same time. They would have never imagined to be traveling in such special company.

After all the passengers had an opportunity to see the relic, it was returned to me. It was not until that moment that I started to think about what was happening. It was as if a movie were playing right before my eyes where events that were not apparently interconnected with each other were taking place. I recalled that I had accompanied John Paul II to Mexico on five occasions. I had not been able to do it with his relic, which to everyone was his sixth trip to Mexico, but at least I was accompanying him on his return trip. I felt, keeping all things in perspective that, sentimentally, it was like returning a loved one's ashes.

*Valentina Alazraki*


## The Traveling Relic in Nigeria

The relic arrived in Lagos, Nigeria on February 19, 2012, thirty years after John Paul II's first visit, his second trip to the African continent and fourteen years after his second visit to Nigeria as part of his tenth trip to Africa.

Providence wanted his arrival to coincide with the inauguration of the Mater Ecclesiae Monastery, born from John Paul II's decision to build a monastery within the Vatican gardens at the beginning of the 1990's, for cloistered nuns from different congregations and countries to live in, rotating every five years. John Paul II had the absolute certainty that the fruitfulness of apostolic life was based upon the strength of prayer. He felt that this monastery in the Vatican gave him the strength to fulfill his apostolic mission the best way possible, bringing grace to the entire world.

John Paul II could have never imagined that his successor would end up living in that monastery; it is fitting that his successor, after becoming the first pontiff in the modern era to resign, has continued his service to the Church and the world precisely through meditation and prayer.

John Paul II could not be absent from that inauguration because he had been the inspiring force behind that reality dedicated to the contemplative life.

During his trip to Nigeria in 1982, John Paul II had encounters with the clergy, and addressed with special warmth the cloistered nuns and monks, to whom he stressed the importance of prayer. The Pope thanked them for their special contributions to the Church and Nigeria's life through the cult of adoration, prayer and contemplation. He encouraged their vocation, convinced that "apostolic fertility is a gift from God," and he told them that united in Christ through prayer, they could obtain grace for both the Church and the entire world. "I trust your support wholeheartedly," John Paul II told them.

This was his first trip following the May 13, 1981 assassination attempt. Many wondered why the Pope, in some way still convalescing, chose to return to Africa, a continent he had visited two years earlier, despite the risks that the trip represented to his still delicate health. The Pope had hinted that in his missionary zeal, he felt the need to continue with his evangelizing mission in the African continent, on behalf of unity among all African Christians.

Both in his first and second visit, John Paul II also built bridges with the Muslims. He told them that ethnic and cultural differences should never be considered motives to justify conflicts. Rather, like the diverse voices in a choir, those differences could co-exist in harmony, as long as there is an authentic desire for mutual respect.

He also affirmed that anytime that violence is exercised in the name of religion, "we must make clear that those cases are not about true religion, for God cannot tolerate violence in His name."

The Archbishop of Lagos, Cardinal Anthony Olubunmi Okongie, who remained impressed by John Paul II's words to the Nigerian contemplatives and his decision ten years later to rely on the prayers of the religious at the Vatican's Mater Ecclesiae Monastery, decided to become the promoter of a similar initiative in Lagos. Thus on February 22, 2004, he canonically erected the Mater Ecclesiae Monastery in his diocese, and for its inauguration on February 2012, he requested the presence of John Paul II's relic.

The driving force behind the Mater Ecclesiae Monastery's construction in Lagos was a woman, Mother Maria Benedicta de Jesus, who would later become the superior of the community. She arrived in Nigeria as a Franciscan missionary, but Providence had provided a turning point in her life. Cardinal Okongie asked her to create a community of religious with a monastic vocation, and to establish rules for the new religious family. For this task, Maria Benedicta was inspired by John Paul II's last encyclical, *Ecclesia de Eucharistia*, which is in a way his doctrinal testament.

Mother understood that with this document, John Paul II had wanted to tell the world that the heart of the Church is prayer, and that Christians have a contemplative vocation. Her mission was to incarnate John Paul II's encyclical, based on his Marian, Eucharistic and ecclesial teachings, into the new monastic life.

In the rich but difficult context of Africa from the point of view of its material and spiritual challenges, the religious would live their vocation as a "divine legend" much appreciated by all Africans and not only the Catholics for whom the cloistered life is the greatest sacred and transcendental expression, because it is the most complete choice of renunciation that a man or woman can make for God and the world. It is also a religious way of life considered tolerant and ecumenical, hence the reason why over the years the monastery became a meeting point for Catholics, Protestants, and even Muslims.

The Mater Ecclesiae Monastery was built on land that had been confiscated from the Church during the dictatorship, and was later returned gratuitously by a Muslim governor. During the relic's stay, another Muslim governor ordered the construction of a road to connect it to the main road. Additionally, the construction of the monastery was made possible thanks to donations from both Christians and Muslims.

The monastery's consecration in February of 2012 coincided with the peaking of religious tensions in the North of the country, where the Christian minority was victim of continuous attacks by Boko Haram's Islamic extremists.

During the preparatory phase of the relic's pilgrimage, Mother Maria Benedicta did not cease to express her concerns about the tense situation that the country was living through. At the same time she had high hopes that it would have the same impact as John Paul II's trips, which had succeeded in bringing about friendship, serenity and confidence in the future.

I accepted to take the relic to Nigeria, because I was convinced that it was very important to do it at that moment in history. It represented a signal that the Nigerian Christian community was not alone; that through John Paul II's blood the universal Church was with them, sharing their suffering and hopes. Many people told me that it would be very unwise, dangerous and risky to take the relic there. I was aware of that, and was indeed afraid, but decided that it was a risk I had to take. *Monsignor Slawomir Oder*

Security measures were very strict and evident during the pilgrimage. These however could not tarnish the festive climate. Thousands of people marched in orderly and respectful fashion to pay homage to the relic. Everyone prayed, many either kissed or touched the ampoule with John Paul II's blood to their foreheads. Mothers holding their children made them touch the reliquary book, and entrusted them to John Paul II.

While watching the procession of the faithful, I remembered the photograph that had been taken of John Paul II while he visited a hut in an African village.

A humble woman had invited him to enter her home. The Pope accepted and sat on a small chair, surrounded by the woman's large family who had offered fruit juice to him, the only gift she could offer. The Pope had accepted humbly, under the worried gaze of his collaborators, who feared for his health given the place's lack of hygiene. The Pope can be seen embracing a child with his right arm, while holding several rosaries with his other hand to give them away as gifts.

John Paul II was the most photographed man in the world, but this is my favorite photograph because it reflects the image of an affectionate father, who is close to humble people and sensitive to their problems. This photograph displays the manner in which he took God even to a lost hut in Africa, naturally and with love. *Monsignor Slawomir Oder*

In the Mater Ecclesiae Monastery, and through his blood, John Paul II was once again among his people, and all those who remembered the warmth and solidarity that he had demonstrated during his two trips.

Suddenly, a tall, elegant and refined black man, dressed with typical Nigerian attire, stopped before the reliquary. His eyes shone, full of tears. He could not stop crying while he leaned forward to kiss the ampoule of John Paul II's blood. They were tears of nostalgia, but also of joy. With a smile, he said in Italian: "We meet again my old and dear friend." He was Nigeria's ambassador at the Vatican during John Paul II's pontificate. *Monsignor Slawomir Oder*

Those few words contained the meaning of the relic's pilgrimage: it was about a presence that does not disappear, is never forgotten, and continues to provoke emotions, awakening feelings of friendship, consolation, and peace.

## The Relic in Colombia

The relic arrived in Colombia on January 2012, twenty-six years after John Paul II's visit. His was a mission of peace in the name of forgiveness due to the violent circumstances that the country was living through. The promoter and true soul behind the initiative was Diana Sofia Giraldo de Melo, an extraordinary woman, full of humanity, journalist, Dean of the Faculty of Mass Media at Bogota's Sergio Arboleda University, and Director of the Visible Victims Foundation. To her, the visit's objective should be to join the blood spilled in Colombia to John Paul II's, as a spiritual reparation offertory for the victims of violence.

The organization of the relic's visit was not easy. The initiative was welcomed with enthusiasm by all of the Colombian bishops at the beginning. Later on, some of them had second thoughts, probably because they did not understand the initiative's true meaning. However, their nuncio, Monsignor Aldo Cavalli, supported Diana Sofia decidedly. The pilgrimage was made possible on a smaller scale than was projected initially, which included all Dioceses, and was limited to Bogota and Cartago.

The first phase took place in the Bogota Cathedral, where thousands of people gathered, many of them closely related to the Visible Victims Foundation. During the celebration, presided by Cardinal Pedro Rubiano Saenz, Bishop Emeritus of Bogota, the emotion could be touched with one's hands, especially during the relic's veneration, accompanied by the testimony of people who had experienced different forms of violence.

I was moved by people's faces who marched before the relic. Mothers whose sons had been taken from them,

children who had lost their parents, victims wounded
in both their hearts and souls. They stopped briefly
to pray silently and intensely before the blood of the
Blessed.                          *Monsignor Slawomir Oder*

A painful cry seemed to be heard inside the Cathedral.
However, the relic reminded everyone of the feeling of forgiveness that had animated John Paul II's life, forgiveness that he had
extended to the Turkish terrorist Mehmet Ali Agca, who came
close to killing him on May 13, 1981. John Paul II's words against
hatred and violence were heard in Bogota's Cathedral. The unforgettable encounter, a fraternal clasp of hands, between John
Paul II and his aggressor, in Rome's Rebibbia jail in 1983 was
recalled. John Paul II clasped the hands of the man that held the
gun that he had fired with the sole purpose of killing him; it was
never known what they told each other during that intense and
impressive colloquy.

Today I have been able to find my aggressor and confirm my forgiveness to him, as I did back on that day
as soon as I was able. We saw each other as persons
and brothers and that all of the events of our lives had
brought us to this brotherhood.

On May 17, 1981, in effect, days after the assassination attempt, and during the prayer of *Regina Coeli* from the Gemelli
Hospital, the Pope, whose voice was still that of someone who
is suffering, pronounced those words that shocked so many
consciences: "I pray for my brother who has wounded me and
whom I forgive sincerely."

From what we know, Ali Agca has never asked for forgiveness for his violent gesture. He has never expressed sincere re-morse. There was a reflection on the Pope's gesture in Bogota's Cathedral, an act that thirty years later continues to raise ques-tions: Why forgive? Why extend a hand to one who tried to kill him? The answer must certainly be found in a desire to be a coherent Christian, to emulate the Master who, while carrying the cross, prayed for his executioners: "Father, forgive them for they know not what they do."

The Pope considered his gesture of forgiving the aggres-sor an initiative from God, and a special grace. He believed that the words he pronounced while inside the ambulance en route to the Gemelli Hospital were "a particular grace from the cru-cified Jesus." He also believed the gesture of forgiveness to be fundamental to building up relationships among men, and de-terminant to mankind's future. He said:

> The act of forgiveness is the first and fundamental
> condition for us men, not to be reciprocally divided
> and confronted against each other as enemies. It is
> fundamental for us to search in God, our Father, for
> togetherness and understanding.

He knew that forgiveness was not easy. It is not something natural or spontaneous to man. "To sincerely forgive, in some cases, could even be heroic," he said. The people gathering in Bogota's Cathedral knew this very well.

The pain of losing a child, brother, parents, or an entire family as a result of war, terrorism, or criminal acts, could lead to total fury towards others. Those who have experienced such a loss cannot avoid feeling the temptation toward hatred and revenge. But John Paul II was convinced that only the warmth of human relations characterized by respect, forgiveness and acceptance can help them overcome such feelings. He believed that a peace process could never be undertaken unless men mature in an attitude of sincere forgiveness. "Without this forgiveness," wrote the Pope, "the wounds will continue to bleed, feeding future generations with a loathing without end and a source of revenge and cause of new ruins. Forgiveness offered and accepted is an indispensable first step in making progress towards an authentic and stable peace."

He was fully aware that forgiveness may seem contrary to human logic, which often obeys the dynamics of challenge and revenge. Forgiveness, however, is inspired by the logic of love, the love that God has for every man and woman, people and nation, as well as the entire human family.

What transpired in the following days was a luminous example that forgiveness and love are stronger than hatred and violence. During the second evening, the relic was placed in the chapel at the national Catholic Television channel, Cristovision. They prayed all night. People tuned to the television channel called to tell about their sorrows. Monsignor Cavalli, Colombia's nuncio, participated in the prayer and commented that the telephones did not stop ringing all night.

On the pilgrimage's third day, the relic was taken to a parish in the Santa Fe neighborhood known as a symbol of degradation, prostitution, drug addiction, and organized crime. Three Polish Pallottine priests have worked in this parish for many years, among them, Father Roman, who was undoubtedly the most moved and excited in front of the relic. The young priest had obvious ambulatory problems: he was dragging one leg and his hand seemed almost immobilized. He was happy to receive the reliquary in his church and had prepared himself with great faith and prayer for this extraordinary event. People were already amassing in the streets adjacent to the parish. There were also a lot of people already at the church's entrance. It was very moving to see Father Roman, despite his physical limitations, and supported by two other priests, kneel to kiss the reliquary.

Accompanied by songs, the procession entered the church. After the reliquary was placed in front of the altar, Father Roman spoke. The attendees could not believe what they were hearing. The priest's voice was identical to John Paul II's. He began to read texts from his teachings, and gave the impression that the Pope was there. In the midst of great emotion, the faithful began to line up to venerate the blood of the Blessed. Their eyes shone with excitement, and everyone seemed to be fully aware of the importance of that moment.

There were families with children, sick people, elderly people, and also many young people whose appearance and demeanor attracted a lot of attention; piercings, tattoos, some of them in a drug induced stupor, transvestites, young women wearing heavy makeup and not properly dressed for a liturgical celebration. Nevertheless, beyond appearances and etiquettes, the procession near the relic reflected the neighborhood's realities, with all its sufferings, contradictions, and marginalization, but above it all its desire for hope and redemption.

While celebrating Mass facing "his Papa's" relic, the young Polish priest saw pass before his eyes the last years of his life. He had arrived in Colombia along with two other priests to take charge of the parish in Santa Fe's barrio.

They were three strong young priests, full of ideals, enthusiasm and faith. They wanted to put that apostolic zeal at the disposition of the faithful, to attempt to rescue those who for a variety of motives had lost their hope and dignity. It didn't take them long, however, to realize that what they had endeavored to do to help young girls abandon a life of prostitution, and youngsters to walk away from drugs and the streets was not succeeding. They began to receive threatening letters with bullets in them, suffer acts of vandalism against the church, as well as physical attacks.

They decided to organize Eucharistic processions through the neighborhood streets, and prayers in the Virgin of Fatima's presence. Despite a negative reaction on the part of those who felt threatened by their initiatives, something began to change among the people. A civic association was born, which proposed Santa Fe's moral revival. Many more of the faithful began to participate in the life of the parish. Then, one day everything changed.

One day, Father Roman suffered a stroke, lost consciousness, and fell to the ground. He remained in a coma for several days. The doctors' prognosis was very negative. He had become a vegetable. He could neither speak nor move. During that time his faithful and colleagues remained by his side, with prayers and much solidarity. His illness touched people's hearts. The doctors did not give up.

After a long therapy, Roman started to move, and gradually to speak, but he was very discouraged. He could not understand why this had happened to him. He saw a very dark future. He felt rage, rebelliousness, and deception. Only his faith helped Roman overcome those moments and avoid falling into despair. Faith and John Paul II's example during his illness were stronger than his discouragement.

By remembering John Paul II's Via Crucis he understood the meaning of suffering as participating in Christ's cross. He understood, and said so with that voice of his identical to John

Paul II's, that pain and sickness are part of humankind's ministry on earth, and must be accepted.

His sufferings and those of the Polish Pope were present before the blood of the Blessed. Father Roman felt like never before the prophetic power of John Paul II's words who, upon leaving the Gemelli Hospital after one of the multiple times he was interned there, affirmed having understood that he had to introduce the Church to the third millennium "with prayer, diverse initiatives, but also with suffering."

# 7 The Beatification

The number of people around the Vatican on May 1, 2011 was impressive. Many had spent the night there. All areas near the Via Della Conciliazione were occupied; the street was completely covered with people along with St. Peter's Square, which had been opened to the public at 5:30 in the morning. Fourteen giant screens had been placed in the city's most important plazas for pilgrims who could not reach St. Peter's Square to follow the most attended beatification in history. The majority of people were content to be in a spot where they could watch the transmission from those screens.

Meanwhile at the Via Della Conciliazione, through which it was impossible to navigate, the faithful prepared for the celebration by singing and praying the chaplet of Divine Mercy revealed to a Polish sister, Saint Faustina, by Jesus Himself. Everyone knew that it was the Sunday of the Divine Mercy, instituted by John Paul II, on the eve of which he had passed away six years earlier. He instituted the Feast when he canonized Faustina Kowalska during the Jubilee of the year 2000. While waiting for the beatification ceremony to begin, selections from John Paul II's homilies where he referred to the Divine Mercy were read.

The entrance procession was particularly solemn and moving; Pope Benedict XVI, wearing John Paul II's chasuble and miter, was visibly moved and happy.

The world's faithful had their eyes set on the central loggia of St. Peter's Basilica on which, back in October 1978, John Paul II had first appeared and with a few improvised words revealed to the world that a totally different pontificate had begun, one which would revolutionize the image of the papacy itself. The new Blessed's tapestry was hanging over the balcony covered with a white cloth.

The beatification rite began with Cardinal Agostino Vallini's formal request. Agostino Vallini, Vicar of the diocese of Rome, asked Benedict XVI to include his beloved predecessor in the catalog of the Blessed. The Cardinal read a brief biography of John Paul II, which was interrupted repeatedly by the faithful's applause. The Cardinal recalled that even though six years had already passed since his death, the recollection, affection, and gratitude of millions of the faithful all over the world for the man who had led the Church for almost twenty-seven years was still very strong. Rome's Vicar placed special emphasis on John Paul II's faith as "deeply rooted and strong, free from fear and compromises, coherent to the last breath, forged by tribulations, fatigue and illness, whose beneficial influence has spread throughout the entire Church, even further, throughout the entire world." He recalled that John Paul II had witnessed dramatic events in the twentieth century, and had always fought to defend the human being, because he believed in humankind, and showed his openness, trust and nearness to them at all times. He also recalled that he had been a man of peace, a builder of hope and above all, one who had loved those "wounded by life," as he called the poor, the sick, the nameless, and the excluded. He recalled his love for young people, for whom he created the World

Youth Day Jubilees that had the objective of making them feel that they were loved and supported in their efforts to build their own future.

Having listened to his Vicar, Benedict XVI pronounced the formula for the beatification:

> Embracing the wishes of our brother Agostino Cardinal Vallini, our Vicar General for the Diocese of Rome, as well as those of many other brothers in the Episcopate and the faithful, after having received the opinion of the Congregation for the Causes of Saints, and by the apostolic authority vested in us, we hereby grant that the Venerable Servant of God John Paul II, Pope, henceforth be called Blessed and that his feast may be celebrated in the places and according to the regulation established by law, every year on October 22.

With these words pronounced in Latin, Benedict elevated his immediate predecessor to the altars; the crowd's enthusiastic shouts were heard in the Square. Among tears of joy, praises and applause, they witnessed the unveiling of the tapestry with the Blessed's smiling face. Some knelt to pray, while others could not contain their tears of emotion. A roaring applause that lasted eight minutes rose from the Square, which seemed a liberating response to a six year wait since cries of "Santo Subito," "Saint Now" were raised from that same place.

Cardinal Agostino Vallini thanked the Pope for the beatification:

> Holy Father, the Vicar General of your Holiness for the Diocese of Rome thanks your Holiness for hav-

ing proclaimed Pope John Paul II, God's venerable servant, Blessed.

Cardinal Vallini, Msgr. Oder and the Pope then exchanged an embrace of peace.

At that moment I heard the vigorous applause that followed Pope Benedict's words back in May 2005 during his meeting with Rome's priests, when he wanted to personally read the document signed by the Cardinal Prefect of the Congregation for the Causes of Saints. In it he communicated his decision to allow the cause for John Paul II's beatification to commence five years earlier than the provisions of the Code of Canon Law allowed. John Paul had returned to the House of the Father only one month earlier.

That reading had a great impact on me, and it made me realize how it reflected Pope Benedict's wishes to respond to the "Santo Subito!" cries that we heard in St. Peter's Square on April 2, 2005.

I recall my surprise and smiled to hear repeated lapses from Pope Benedict in which he referred to John Paul II as "our dear Pope," when in reality he was the Pope and John Paul was his "beloved predecessor." Twenty-three years of collaboration, friendship, affection, and loyalty cannot be erased simply with a stroke of a pen. That day at the Basilica of St. John Lateran we all, Pope Benedict included, had the feeling that John Paul was in our midst. Even at that moment I did not know that my life was about to make an extraordinary turn. One hour later, Cardinal

Camillo Ruini, the Pope's Vicar to the City of Rome, made me aware that I would be the postulator of John Paul II's beatification cause.

Six years later, on May 1, 2011, I heard the echo from the applause with which the priests had received the announcement that the cause for beatification had begun when Pope Benedict, visibly moved and full of joy exclaimed almost shouting: "John Paul II is Blessed."

Music from the hymn composed by Marco Frisina accompanied the unveiling of the tapestry with John Paul II's face, which smiled to the hundreds of thousands of faithful who had arrived from all over the world.

I will never forget the penetrating and joyful gaze with which Pope Benedict looked at me when we exchanged an embrace of peace. I remember the strength of his hands when he raised me up after I had knelt before him. Nor will I ever forget the words that he whispered in my ear while he pressed me with a strength superior to what I imagined a man his age would have. Those were the most personally gratifying words I had received since the process began. When I turned around and began to step down from the altar zone, I saw a Church that was in a festive mood, with thousands of faithful from all nationalities with flags, and banners in different languages. I had the impression that after the Pope's embrace, I was receiving the entire Church's embrace. Tears leapt up. It was a liberating moment for me.

The intense work of the last six years, both good

and bad moments, nights spent at my desk, intercontinental trips, exhaustion, stress, the tensions leading to the beatification, misunderstandings, humiliations, which hurt even more because they had been inflicted by people whom I trusted, the constant pressure from the press always asking: "When is the beatification going to happen?", all magically disappeared. Everything was finished, at least for the moment.

During the process, which seemed long to me even though it was one of the briefest in history, my motto was the phrase that Pope Benedict pronounced when he received me along with the Polish bishops during their *ad limina* visit, a visit that bishops make to the Vatican every five years. In that occasion he told me: "Work fast, but work well." From that moment on, his words accompanied me throughout the layered process. I also knew that he was praying both for my collaborators and me. He himself said so several times, like during the commemorations of John Paul II's death or during his visit to Cracow, when he looked out the Archbishop's window in Franciszkanska Street, from which his predecessor had looked out so many times before. It was important for me to know that Pope Benedict was praying for me. I also felt that John Paul II was doing so as well. He always believed that the solutions to many problems could be found in prayer.

I could see the power of prayer during the beatification process, especially during difficult moments when it seemed that insurmountable obstacles would get in our way. I felt the strength of prayer from the faithful around the world, who created prayer groups over the internet. Several contemplative monasteries welcomed my invitation to create a sort of a monastery online, where the faithful could leave their intentions, requests for grace, and their desire for John Paul II to become Blessed.

During the beatification I remembered the first letters I received informing me about a grace received. I remember the emotion I felt when I read one from New Zealand, and another from Vladivostok, Russia.

When I saw so many thousands of faithful gathered at St. Peter's Square, and around the Vatican, it became evident to me that the missionary Pope had sowed a lot of seeds of love, fraternity, and peace during his apostolic trips. He had defended the poor and the weakest of the weak; he had given voice to those who lacked the right to make theirs heard; he consoled the afflicted; in other words, he had disseminated much hope. Now, in this emotional ceremony, the faithful were responding to him with love and gratitude.

I knew that prayer groups to pray for and remember John Paul II, his gestures and words, had been born in all continents without distinction. I understood that people were still thirsty to listen to his teaching, wanted to imitate his Eucharistic and Marian example, and to be inspired by his generosity and works of fraternal charity.

During the beatification I had the impression I was participating in the joy of the entire Church, the joy of Pope Benedict, the faithful, of the impressive number of official delegations that, beyond their political or religious realities, wanted to be present to thank the Polish Pope for the closeness he had with them, as well as the efforts he made to tear down walls and build bridges. For them, to participate in the beatification was "a duty of justice."

For me as a Polish person, and son of the same nation as Karol Wojtyla, the beatification was also a patriotic experience.

Contrary to his predecessors, John Paul II was not afraid to express his relationship with his own nation. He felt closely linked to its history, past and present. He shared our hopes during his pontificate, our wish for liberty; he cried for his compatriots' suffering and encouraged positive aspirations to liberty, justice and solidarity. He always invited us to be faithful to the values of our forefathers in the faith, and to the glorious memory of those who had fought for liberty. The grandiosity of his heart and magnanimity were demonstrated through his ability to manifest his love of country in the countries and nations he visited during almost twenty-seven years.

The flags from all over the world at St. Peter's Square were proof that his relationship with Poland and his Polish identity never represented a limit or an obstacle to his paternal love and pastoral commitment that embraced the entire world. To the contrary; his profound sense of belonging and deep roots to his nation's healthiest traditions made him sensible to the aspirations of all peoples. It made him learn to appreciate their diversity and identity, because their

collective whole makes up the Church's cultural richness, which speaks in different languages throughout
the world, but asks for the same justice and dignity.

During the beatification, with many people of different races and cultures present, I felt the universal
paternity that John Paul II had exercised. It was about
a paternity that, coming from a country that had to
fight to defend the Catholic Church, the heart of
their national identity, against the prepotent presence
of Marxist forces, had crossed borders and could not
speak to the world with detachment and diplomatic
coldness. During the process, I was moved to confirm that his words of encouragement to the Polish
people were received with respect and hope by others. Somehow they made them their own and made
them aware of their rights and historical responsibilities. The birth of the Solidarity movement was the
first piece of that reality, which with domino effect
made inhuman and unjust regimes disappear in all of
Eastern Europe, to reach the historic moment of the
fall of the Berlin Wall, and the reunification of the
two Germanies.

Many moments of my youth passed through my
mind during the ceremony, when looking at the darkness of a country oppressed by a regime that was
alien to our culture, our history, our conscience, it
seemed that our future was grey, sad, poor, marked
by a struggle for survival. Liberty only existed in our
dreams, and the only place where there was enough
space for its realization was in the churches.

John Paul II's election suddenly made us rise out

of the darkness. Heaven opened up and life returned; churches were once again full of promise and prophecy. We were no longer condemned to darkness and mediocrity. A few months after his election, John Paul II traveled to Poland and, among the other things he told us, I recall that he pronounced words that marked my life. In an encounter with us, young people thirsty to hear words of hope, John Paul II told us that we were to always be demanding with ourselves, for one has to be demanding with oneself even when no one is asking anything of us. Those words were an imperative to me, a ticket to a better world, the way to be able to change a reality that seemed eternal.

During his trip to Poland in 1987, he spoke about this once again when referring to the battle of Westerplatte, a piece of land by the Baltic Sea where a group of young Polish soldiers, under the command of Major Henryk Sucharski, resisted in a hopeless battle against the aggressor. John Paul II said: "You too, young friends, will find your Westerplatte in life, in other words, a just cause for which one cannot avoid fighting, duties, obligations that must be met. There are situations from which one cannot run away, where a series of values must be maintained and defended against and around oneself."

On beatification day and upon stepping down from the Basilica's atrium on my way towards St. Peter Square, I heard those words once again. I was seeing those events right before me, and my heart rejoiced to see that multicolored multitude, to see so many flags from European countries and the entire world, among which the red and white colors of Poland's flag stood out. I saw a free people that rejoiced in celebrating a new Blessed, prophet of true liberty. Sanctity is true liberty; it is an "assumed and carried out" mission. It is "a known, maintained, defended and lived truth."

Sanctity, like liberty, does not know barriers of language, ethnicity, or race. It speaks a common language. At that moment, I was happy to be Catholic. I was proud to be Polish.     *Monsignor Slawomir Oder*

On that day, another priest was also proud to be Polish. One of Pope Benedict's Masters of Ceremonies during the beatification was Polish Monsignor Konrad Krajewski. Six years earlier, he had been put in charge of taking the Gospel and placing it over John Paul II's coffin the day of his funeral in that same Square. His emotion was very strong and obvious. He recalled that as he carried the Gospel, he only thought about doing it in a dignified manner.

I wanted to do it as one carries life's most important book; John Paul II's life. I felt undignified about such gesture of leaving that most important book of light on his coffin. I felt so small and such a sinner, and asked God for the wisdom to carry it in my life as John Paul II did.

After John Paul II was officially declared Blessed, Mother Tobiana, the Polish sister who had cared for him with extraordinary love and dedication until the end of his life, and the French sister Marie Simon-

Pierre, favored by the Blessed with her healing from Parkinson's, presented the reliquaries, two small tubes with John Paul II's blood, placed inside a chest, which in some way seemed to emulate details from the inside of the Divine Mercy's Polish sanctuary.

Mary Simon-Pierre had arrived in Rome with some seven hundred pilgrims from the Aix en Provence and Arles Dioceses; there were twenty-five Little Sisters of Les Petites Sœurs des Maternités Catholiques, or Catholic Motherhood. On the day of the beatification she arrived at St. Peter's Square very early. Next to her was a guardian Angel, Angelo, who guided her among the people and allowed her to pass by saying the magic words to the Vatican guards: "She is the religious from John Paul's miracle." The guards looked intently at her and, visibly moved, would say, *Avanti, Avanti,* "go ahead, go ahead."

"I was profoundly impressed to see the ocean of people moving towards the Square," Marie Simon-Pierre observed. "You could see flags from all over the world, everyone was singing; they were going to a party."

It rained a little at first on that day. She went to the Basilica and there she had an unforgettable encounter with Mother Tobiana.

There were no words between us, just a very intense look that said everything. I knew that she was the woman who had cared for John Paul II with extraordinary devotion. She knew that I was the instrument that God had utilized for John Paul to become Blessed. We were both granted an enormous privilege: both of us could be alone to venerate the Pope's reliquary.

Side by side, the two women took part in the beatification ceremony. Mother Tobiana was tasked with taking John Paul II's relic to Pope Benedict: Sister Marie Simon-Pierre was tasked with taking it to the Square. With Mother Tobiana next to her, Sister Marie Simon-Pierre walked towards Pope Benedict and later descended before the crowd.

> To be able to kneel before Pope Benedict, see his warm smile, receive the relic from Sister Tobiana's hands, was a moment of grace.

Marie Simon-Pierre felt very light on her feet, deeply moved, aware of that moment of grace. She felt submerged in that multitude that did not cease to express their joy.

> I was in the middle of that multitude, and John Paul II was holding my hand. It was as if he said to me: "Go ahead, don't be afraid. You have believed and now you see the glory of God."

The glory of God had made possible her healing from Parkinson's, an illness for which there is no cure, and now she was there as an involuntary protagonist to the beatification of the Pope who had been an example of suffering for her to follow, a pastor and a man, an apostle of prayer and mercy.

At that moment she could not describe what it meant to her to see raised to the altars the Pope that she had admired for his closeness to the neediest, the weakest of the weak, and the sick. She had admired his life, strength, courage, and humility. She recalled how his example had been determinant for her to face her illness. Thanks to him she even loved her illness, for understanding the meaning of pain translated into participating in the cross of Christ.

While Pope Benedict celebrated Mass, she recalled that her miraculous healing was not only of her body, but of her soul as well. For her to heal had been like being born again, but her spiritual life had also been shaken up; after her healing she had initiated a new spiritual life.

In those moments she perceived the depth of the mystery surrounding her healing, became totally attached to the Eucharist, to Eucharistic adoration, and to the prayer of the rosary that John Paul II promoted throughout the world.

She recalled that on that day after her miracle, she wrote to her parents to give them the news of her inexplicable healing with these words:

> To God, nothing is impossible. If you believe, you will see. The Lord has healed me through John Paul II's intercession. He granted me that grace on June 2nd. I believe this is best anniversary gift that I can give you.

That day was her parents' anniversary. She also recalled that she had shared with the Little Sisters of the Catholic Motherhood the conviction that the miracle that John Paul II had granted to her was a signal that the Pope wanted to give to the congregation, to families, to mothers, and all those who work on behalf of human life. Sister Marie Simon-Pierre, who currently dedicates herself to the care of the sick afflicted with Parkinson's, also continues to care for mothers and their babies, being faithful to her apostolate in favor of life, following John Paul II's footsteps.

For the postulation of the cause for beatification, the fact that this religious sister suffered from Parkinson's, just like John

Paul II, was no coincidence. It was a sign from Providence because, through his intercession, a woman dedicated to life was healed. Her healing represented another piece of the magnificent mosaic of the Gospel of Life, of which John Paul II was its great promoter.

Meanwhile, as the beatification ceremony continued, Sister Mary Simon-Pierre read the prayer that the Little Sisters of the Catholic Motherhood had written after her healing:

> Father, from the window of your house, John Paul II sees and blesses us all. May his smile over humanity reveal his sanctity to all men. In your mercy and through his intercession, you have cast your glance upon our institute through Sister Marie Simon-Pierre's healing. If it be your will, may this bestowal of mercy represent a small stone in the cause of the beatification of the man who offered his own illness to redeem the world.

After months of struggle against a disease that worsened in parallel with the Pope's last moments of life, she remembered the exhaustion and the weakness she felt on April 2, 2011, when John Paul II died.

On the afternoon of April 2, the entire community had gathered for the prayer vigil in St. Peter's Square, retransmitted live by the Paris Diocese through French television. Together they heard the news about John Paul II's death. At that moment, the entire world had collapsed on top of her. She had lost the friend who understood her and gave her strength to keep going. In the following days she had the sensation of a great void, but also the certainty about his living presence.

Beginning on May 13th, the Feast of Our Lady of Fatima, a day in which Pope Benedict XVI announced a five year dispensation to begin the cause of beatification for John Paul II, sisters from all French and African communities began to pray for her healing, through John Paul II's intercession. They prayed incessantly, until they received the news about her recovery.

She recalled that during those months she kept hearing an inner voice that said: *"If you believe, you will see the glory of God."* Then, on June 1st, she could take it no more; she struggled to remain standing and walk. In the afternoon of the next day, she went looking for her Mother Superior to ask her for permission to work in the hospital. She encouraged her to resist a little longer until her return from Lourdes in August, and added: "John Paul II has not said the last word yet." Hours later, and inexplicably, she was healed. During the beatification ceremony, she asked herself once more as to how one cannot believe before such a great mystery.

Mixed feelings could be read on Mother Tobiana's face. On one hand, the joy of having seen the man whom she assisted for so many years elevated to the honor of the altars; on the other, the pain which was not overcome by his death, even though she knew that John Paul II was in Heaven. She was the last person to hear his weak voice, the one to whom he expressed his desire to go to the house of the Father.

There is no better example of love and dedication than that of Mother Tobiana. Not one word about her long years of service at John Paul II's side ever came out of her mouth. Those of us who were privileged to see her in private, and away from the spotlight after John Paul II's death, could perceive her suffering, expressed through silent tears during celebrations in memory of the Polish Pope. She had been his shadow day and night. When he did not go to sleep, she would sit on a chair next to John Paul II's bed, whether in the Vatican or on a trip, and not move from his side, with her gaze fixed upon him, vigilant that his sleep not be interrupted by any of his multiple health problems.

Not a single complaint ever came out of her mouth about not being able to rest, the tension and stress that never abandoned her, the pain that she felt in confronting John Paul II's ailments. Apparently frail on the surface, she had been a strong woman. Upon seeing her come down from the altar towards the Square after having taken the reliquary, John Paul II's physicians recalled the manner in which she was able to convince the Pope about the usefulness of a particular treatment when he resisted it, afraid that it could diminish his capacity to be near his faithful. They recalled her discretion, her silence, her gentleness, but above all, her determination to treat a sometimes difficult patient who always thought about his mission first, and his health second.

Upon greeting her, Pope Benedict looked at her with affection and gratitude; he seemed to want to thank her in the name of the hundreds of thousands of faithful who were gathering there at that moment, for the way in which she had cared for and assisted his predecessor; with love, humility and a devotion about which she never boasted. We could notice the Pope's appreciation through the greetings they exchanged. After John Paul II's death, the Pope had the opportunity to see her year after year at the Masses he celebrated to commemorate his death. They had also seen each other in Poland, during Pope Benedict's visit to that country to pay tribute to his predecessor's memory.

Despite the pain over her loss, she, along with all of John Paul II's closest collaborators, felt fortunate that, at the moment of his death and without thinking, they had sung a Te Deum of thanks for the gift they had received of having been able to share so many years of their lives with one who to them had been above all, a man of God, a man whom they had often seen in contact with God through prayer.

Back at her seat again, Mother Tobiana recalled the way in which John Paul II, who seemed to pray for the entire world every day, prayed. She remembered that on one occasion she asked him to pray for her mother. He had looked at her almost surprised at her petition, and responded: "I pray for her every day."

After the reliquaries were delivered, the hymn *Gloria in excelsis* was sung, followed by the Prayer of the Faithful for Divine Mercy Sunday, and the Liturgy of the Word. The first reading was read in Polish; the Psalm was read in Latin; the second reading was read in English; and the Gospel was proclaimed in Latin. Afterwards, Benedict XVI gave his homily, in which he, visibly moved, praised the sanctity of his predecessor. The words he pronounced with such strength and great satisfaction were unforgettable: "É Beato!" "He is Blessed!"

The German pontiff, who at that moment was eighty-four years of age, explained that it had been his wishes for the beatification process to take place "fairly quickly," because even during John Paul II's funeral the "aroma of his beatitude" was perceivable.

Today the much anticipated day has arrived. This day has arrived quickly because the Lord so wished it.

Six years ago we gathered in this Square to celebrate the funeral of Pope John Paul II. Our grief at his loss was deep, but even greater was our sense of an immense grace which embraced Rome and the whole world: a grace which was in some way the fruit of my beloved predecessor's entire life, and especially of his witness in suffering. Even then we perceived the fragrance of his sanctity, and in any number of ways God's People showed their veneration for him. For this reason, with all due respect for the Church's canonical norms, I wanted his cause of beatification to move forward with reasonable haste. And now the longed-for day has come; it came quickly, because this is what was pleasing to the Lord: John Paul II is blessed!

In referring to his predecessor, Pope Benedict highlighted that: "this model son of the Polish nation helped Christians throughout the world to not be afraid to call themselves Christian, to belong to the Church and proclaim the Gospel."

What the newly-elected Pope asked of everyone, he was himself the first to do: society, culture, political and economic systems he opened up to Christ, turning back with the strength of a titan – a strength which came to him from God – a tide which appeared irreversible. By his witness of faith, love and apostolic courage, accompanied by great human charisma, this exemplary son of Poland helped believers throughout the world not to be afraid to be called Christian, to belong to the Church, to speak of the Gospel.

The Pope demonstrated his joy because the beatification was taking place on the first day of the "Marian month, under Mary's maternal gaze, who with her faith sustains the faith of the apostles, and continually sustains that of their successors," and for having been John Paul II's collaborator for some twenty-six years.

Finally, on a more personal note, I would like to thank God for the gift of having worked for many years with Blessed Pope John Paul II. I had known him earlier and had esteemed him, but for twenty-three years, beginning in 1982 after he called me to Rome to be Prefect of the Congregation for the Doctrine of the Faith, I was at his side and came to revere him all the more. My own service was sustained by his spiritual depth and by the richness of his insights. His example of prayer continually impressed and edified me: he remained deeply united to God even amid the many demands of his ministry.

Then too, there was his witness in suffering: the Lord gradually stripped him of everything, yet he remained a "rock," as Christ desired. His profound humility, grounded in close union with Christ, enabled him to continue to lead the Church and to give to the world a message which became all the more eloquent as his physical strength declined. In this way he lived out in an extraordinary way the vocation of every priest and bishop to become completely one with Jesus, whom he daily receives and offers in the Church.

What was most moving was that, visibly moved, Pope Benedict, improvising, asked the new Blessed to bless him: "You have blessed us from this Square so many times. Holy Father, today we beg you, bless us. Amen."

To listen to Pope Benedict almost implore the Holy Father, deceased six years earlier, for his blessing, moved me a great deal. I was moved by the affection and veneration, as he himself qualified it, for his predecessor. I was impressed by his sensitivity, fragility, humility, almost stepping aside so that St. Peter's Square could be John Paul II's Square, just as it had been for twenty-six years. That day I thought that perhaps we had not been able to understand Pope Benedict because the memory, and even the presence of John Paul II, had been too strong during those six years.

I recalled a prayer vigil that took place at that same Square the night before the first anniversary of John Paul's death. Tens of thousands of faithful, full of nostalgia, prayed the rosary, John Paul II's favorite prayer. Pope Benedict was standing in a corner of the window of his private study. There was the impression that he wanted to be invisible, that he did not want to impose his presence in any way.

Throughout those six years, John Paul II's figure had accompanied me constantly, both in my professional and personal life.

I recalled that shortly after his death, I received a letter inviting me to be one of the witnesses in the cause of John Paul II's beatification. I never imagined that this could happen one day, despite the fact that I followed him from the first to the last day of his pontificate, having accompanied him in one hundred trips throughout the world.

I got in touch with the Postulator's Office for the cause. Over the course of two sessions, they asked me one hundred and twenty questions about the manner in which John Paul II had lived all the virtues.

That was the beginning of a collaboration that lasts to this day. In making the decision to write a book about the cause for his beatification I relied on the help, and especially the friendship, of all the people who had made John Paul II's beatification possible. It seemed to me that, although invisible, I contributed a little grain of sand to that beatification, and that perception increased my emotion.

This ceremony was like the end of a long trip that started thirty-three years earlier, when I was given the job of covering the election of the first non-Italian Pope in more than five hundred years. I recalled the manner in which luck, or Providence, had woven its web in having John Paul II choose Mexico as the first stop of his traveling pontificate, immediately transforming him into a Mexican Pope, enamored of Mexico, of its inhabitants, their joy, and faith. I recalled all the times that at first, when he saw me, he would point his finger at me and say: "Mexico, Mexico," the way in which he learned my name little by little, and always had a gesture or caress for me, which were somehow and symbolically intended for all Mexicans who had fallen in love with him, and had accompanied him throughout his entire pontificate.

I recall those moments in which as a journalist, I had the certainty of being witness to historical events: the day he fell bloodied inside the jeep in which he toured St. Peter's Square, under the bullets of Turkish terrorist Mehmet Ali Agca, who had fired convinced he would kill him. I recall his weak voice from the Gemelli Hospital, when from his bed, he forgave the man who had sought his life. I recalled all the times I had entered and exited that hospital, especially the last two hospitalizations before his death. I remember the day he appeared in the window of his room up on the tenth floor with a cannula in his neck after he had undergone a tracheotomy; the day he appeared in his private studio's window at the Apostolic Palace on Easter Sunday to give his blessing, and could not utter one word. I remember the manner in which he struck the lectern to share his frustration and impotence with the faithful who were present. I remember the last Wednesday that I saw him alive, three days before his death; with a superhuman effort, he got up from the bed in which he was agonizing, dressed as Pope in his white cassock; with both the cannula in his neck and another for his intravenous feeding, he appeared in the window that had been his for the last twenty-six and a half years for the last time. He knew it was Wednesday and that the Square was full of pilgrims because it was a General Audience day. He did not want to deprive them by his absence. He remained at the window only for a few seconds, with a face of suffering that I will never forget. With obvious effort, he attempted to outline a silent blessing and retired. The emotion at the Square was enormous. We all knew that we would not see him again, and that he wanted to bid goodbye to each one of us. We were profoundly moved and grateful at the same time for his devotion until the very end.

Three days later, on that unforgettable Saturday April 2nd, I heard the voice of my daughter Carolina telling me: "Mother, the Pope has died," minutes prior to beginning the transmission in which we would announce that John Paul II had returned to the House of the Father. I saw myself following the route of the catafalque with John Paul II from the Apostolic Palace to St. Peter's Square and later to the Basilica under the astonished gaze of thousands of people who at that moment felt profoundly like orphans. I saw myself inside St. Peter's Basilica, hiding my tears when they allowed a group of journalists to pass to be able to bid goodbye to John Paul II. I remember the day of his funeral, the book of the Gospel lying on his coffin that, due to the strong wind, suddenly closed shut; the moment the coffin was raised and, before entering the Basilica for the last time, being turned towards what had been his Square for more than a quarter century.

I felt ashamed for the sadness I felt as I witnessed Pope Benedict's first general audience, when I saw him enter through the rear door of the hearings area, through which I had become accustomed to see John Paul II enter in his wheelchair. I was also ashamed about the feeling of orphanhood that had accompanied me during those six years, by not getting used to the fact that Pope Benedict, and not John Paul II, traveled in the papal aircraft. In the midst of the joy and emotion of recognizing something that was within reach, especially in the last part of John Paul II's life, marked by a strength and devotion that were truly heroic, I felt affection for Pope Benedict, and admiration for his profound humility. While I looked at John Paul II's photograph taken in 1995 when he was seventy-five years old, in which he looked happy, with a youthful air about him and a smile in his eyes, I thought that John Paul II knew very well what he was doing when in his book *Rise, Let Us Be on Our Way* he wrote that to him, Cardinal Joseph Ratzinger had been a sure friend whom he could trust.

*Valentina Alazraki*

After the homily, the Pope read the Prayers of the Faithful in multiple languages; the petitions had been drafted based upon the Latin words that gave name to the new Blessed's encyclicals.

Cardinal Stanislaw Dziwisz, the man who had been John Paul II's secretary for forty years, surely the man who knew him well, appreciated him and experienced his personal sanctity the most, was sitting in the front row.

Hours earlier, when celebrating a solemn prayer vigil, the Cardinal had moved tens of thousands of faithful gathered at the Circus Maximus to prepare for the beatification, by affirming that if Pope Benedict had decided to beatify him, it was because he was already a saint in life. He recalled that John Paul II was in love with God, who only asked him to leave him the space, time and silence to be with God; who knew how to lose himself in God anywhere, under any condition; even when he was studying, or among people, he did so very naturally. He also shared his memories of the last days of John Paul II's earthly life.

Like a biblical patriarch, he prepared us for the separation, holding us by the hand, focused on what he was doing. He would die like an exhausted, and at the same time lucid, fighter: "Here I am death; you will have me only for an instant. I am going home, to my Mother and Father, where I have always longed to go. That is where life is, and where one is truly Blessed forever."

Not far from Cardinal Stanislaw Dziwisz was Joaquin Navarro Valls, John Paul II's spokesman for more than twenty years. In those moments he too thought that saints are already so during their lives, or they are not.

With great emotion, he recalled the serene moments, the historical moments, the joyful moments he had lived at John Paul II's side; but above all the sad moments came to mind, the difficult moments in recent times, when for a smile to return to his face, expressionless because of his Parkinson's illness, Navaro Valls would wear a red clown's nose. The effect was immediate, and John Paul II outlined a smile.

He recalled the tears he could not hold back when during one of the last press conferences he held prior to John Paul II's death a journalist surprisingly asked him what his personal feelings about John Paul II's agony were. He had to stand up and conclude the press conference.

While giving testimony during the prayer vigil at the Circus Maximus the evening prior to the beatification, Navarro Valls remembered that the most beautiful teaching he had received from John Paul II was respect for the human being, in which he saw God's image. He had decided that his pontificate's priority was to preserve the transcendent character of the individual, because in today's world we run the risk of being treated like a thing, an object.

"When you live next to someone like him," he added, "this

respect is something you never forget." Visibly moved, the ex-spokesman wanted to publicly express his gratitude to John Paul II: "Thank you John Paul II for the masterpiece that, thanks to God's help, your life was."

Sitting near them was Doctor Renato Buzzonetti, John Paul II's physician, who signed the Pope's death certificate. The Pope had been his patient for some twenty-six years and at whose side he lived terribly dramatic moments. He recalled the manner in which John Paul II demonstrated a total abandonment to God's will, from the very first difficult moment they lived together.

> This could be observed during his illnesses, the small and the important ones; he put himself in the Lord's hands, and bore everything like a cross that only he could carry.

During the ceremony, Doctor Buzzonetti recalled that after the terrible hours that followed the May 13, 1981 assassination attempt, the most difficult moment for him was not in 1992 when he had to tell John Paul II about a tumor in his colon that had to be removed, but the brief conversation he had with him in the Gemelli Hospital on February 2005, after it was decided to tell him that he had to undergo a tracheotomy, and that more than likely he could never be able to speak again.

> That was a severe blow to the Pope. He had already lost his ability to gesture, to be able to walk, to be able to change positions in bed. Now he would lose the capability to talk. To him this was really the last nail in his cross.

During John Paul II's beatification, Doctor Buzzonetti never doubted the sanctity of his patient. He was surprised by his physical fragility, coupled with his greatness as a man of God and his profound serenity. He commented that:

> His supernatural vision of life was his charisma; he did not allow the small or great difficulties that he undoubtedly had to face during the years of his pontificate to either defeat or distract him.

Pope Benedict concelebrated the beatification Mass with all the Cardinals present in Rome, and with Monsignor Mieczyslaw Mokrzycj, who was John Paul II's secretary during the last years of his life. During the Eucharistic liturgy, a Polish young man and a Polish young woman, visibly moved and dressed with their typical Polish attire, started the offertory procession and approached the Pope. After the solemn blessing the new Blessed's official hymn was sung.

The joy and jubilation of the ceremony were followed by moments of sadness when the doors of the Basilica opened allowing the faithful to pass by and pay homage to John Paul II's remains, as had occurred in the days following his death.

John Paul II's coffin was placed before the Basilica's Altar of the Confession. A facsimile of the Lorch Gospels, of medieval times, that contains the Gospels of St. Luke and St. John and is one of the most heavily guarded books in the Vatican's Apostolic Library, was placed on top of it.

It was open and supported by a pillow embroidered with gold ornaments, along with a flower arrangement with the Vatican colors: yellow and white.

Provision had been made for people to parade before the

coffin until 7:00 P.M. the next day, to allow as many pilgrims through as possible.

Two days earlier, the coffin had been taken from the tomb it had occupied in the Vatican Grottos, located a few meters from the chapel dedicated to the Virgin of Guadalupe that John Paul II had built in 1992 so that there would be a "prolongation of the experience of Tepeyac," and placed next to St. Peter's tomb.

The first to enter the Basilica was Pope Benedict, who knelt on a kneeler before his predecessor's coffin, which remained closed. He was followed by the cardinals, bishops, priests, heads of delegations and finally, the faithful from all over the world.

Among the people who venerated John Paul II's mortal remains were all those who had somehow been his family in the Vatican.

Some relived the pain of April 2, 2005, the arrangements during the following days, the funeral celebrated on April 8, and finally the placement of his coffin in the Vatican Grottos.

I was profoundly moved to see Monsignor Piero Marini, who had been his Master of Ceremonies for eighteen years and who, along with his secretary Stanislaw Dziwisz, had been given the task of covering John Paul II's face with a white veil. "It was a sign that the Pope had left us forever," explained Monsignor Marini.

During the last years of John Paul II's life, Monsignor Piero Marini, the man responsible for all liturgical celebrations, never separated himself from him; he constantly monitored the Pope's movements with attentive and worried eyes; on several occasions he was able to prevent John Paul II from either slipping or falling. For example, as it happened in the Sistine Chapel or during his last trip to Lourdes, while kneeling in the grotto of apparitions, he was on the verge of falling.

Monsignor Marini recalled all the Pope's suffering moments, his aching body, the numerous times he placed a small pillow on the back of his chair because of the sores he had developed as a result of his posture. Monsignor Marini did not know about those sores because John Paul II never complained until the nuns who washed the linen noticed blood on the sheets and witnessed the manner in which the Pope suffered.

While paying homage to his remains, as he had six years earlier in that heartbreaking farewell in the Vatican Grottos when he closed the coffin, Monsignor Marini recalled that in 1998 he had been given the task of writing a Pope's funeral rites. John Paul II approved it. He even wanted to sign the text but Stanislaw told him that it was not necessary. Of course, he knew that it would be the rite with which he would be buried.

In passing before the coffin, Monsignor Marini recalled the last time he saw John Paul II alive.

> I caressed him, and told him: "Holy Father pray for me, pray for the Church." He raised his hands from the mattress. At first I did not understand the gesture, but later understood that he wanted to greet me with his body. He squeezed my hand and we remained there, I don't know for how long, a few seconds, but it was like an eternity. I always remember that hand which held mine, and expect this beatification, these memories, to remain all my life.

# 8 John Paul II and Benedict XVI

On February 28, 2013, when Benedict XVI boarded the helicopter that would take him from the Vatican Gardens to the Castelgandolfo residence, where two hours later he would cease to be Pope, unprecedented in modern history, there were many mixed feelings in his heart; joyful and sad memories, yearnings, questions, and unknowns about his future life as the first Emeritus Pope.

While flying over the city of Rome, of which he had been bishop for the past eight years, in the midst of feelings and emotions, he was saddened to think that he was not going to be the Pope who would canonize his predecessor.

However, in the course of such a significant day for him and for the history of the Church, he had received news that gave him a lot of joy and that somehow mitigated the sadness that he felt upon abandoning the Vatican, after publicly announcing that he no longer possessed the strength to continue to guide at the helm of the Church. On that day he was informed of the approval by the Commission of Theologians, with prior approval by the Doctors' Commission of the Congregation for the Causes of Saints, of the miracle that would make John Paul II a saint. In an intimate conversation, he acknowledged that during those difficult hours, the news had given much consolation and great joy to him.

We believe that this circumstance reflects the essence of the special relationship between John Paul II and Benedict XVI more than a thousand words could do.

At first sight, it would seem difficult that someone from Poland, a man of action, extroverted, master of communication and broad gestures, charismatic, with the overwhelming force of a crusader, and a German, intellectual, methodic theologian, introverted, thinker, little loving of facing large crowds, could establish a profound friendship.

Beyond their apparent differences, then Cardinal Joseph Ratzinger and John Paul II succeeded. Friendship united them from the day they met until the Polish Pope's last day. Pope Emeritus Benedict XVI's veneration for his predecessor continues to this day.

In his book *Rise, Let Us Be on Our Way*, John Paul II made that friendship public with recognition that he did not extend to other collaborators: "I thank God for Cardinal Ratzinger's presence and help. He is a sure friend," wrote the Pope.

Years later, in his book *The Light of the World*, Pope Benedict XVI revealed that when he was about to be seventy-five years old, the date upon which he had to present his resignation to the Pope, John Paul II told him that it was not necessary for him to write that letter. "I want to continue to have you with me until the end," he told him. And so it happened in spite of the two occasions on which Cardinal Ratzinger expressed to John Paul II his desire to leave his post as prefect of the Congregation for the Doctrine of the Faith to return to his life of study and reading that he remained on.

To the German journalist who interviewed him for *The*

*Light of the World,* Pope Benedict commented: "He had placed a very profound and cordial confidence in me; it was, so to speak, like a guarantee that we would remain on the right course for the faith."

Theirs was an encounter between two men who had forged their faith and intelligence in the course of two tragic situations of the twentieth century, Marxism and Nazism, between two men anchored in tradition, free spirits, lovers of beauty, of God and the human being. They did not always agree with each other, but always respected each other. In his book *Salt of the Earth,* Cardinal Ratzinger recognized that they did disagree on some points, but gave assurances that he never disobeyed him.

Cardinals Karol Wojtyla and Joseph Ratzinger, sons of two nations that in history were enemies, met during the meetings that preceded the two conclaves that took place in the summer of 1978. Cardinal Wojtyla knew about the German Cardinal's theological stature, who in turn knew about the Polish Cardinal's philosophical preparation.

In celebration of the twenty-seventh anniversary of John Paul II's election, and before Polish television cameras, Pope Benedict XVI told about the beginning of a friendship that would last until the end of the Polish Pope's life, whose memory would forever mark the German Pope.

> I felt a great sympathy for him from the beginning, and thanks to God the then Cardinal gave me his friendship from the start, undeserved from my perspective. I am grateful for the trust he gave me, without any merit. Additionally, I was impressed with his cordiality, without prejudice, with which he found me. A great friendship emerged from the heart, without a lot of words.

Joaquin Navarro Valls, John Paul II's spokesman, witnessed many encounters between Cardinal Ratzinger and John Paul II. "To listen to them was an extraordinary experience, because the Cardinal contributed his theological vision while John Paul II contributed his philosophical point of view."

From their first encounters, Cardinal Ratzinger was impacted by Cardinal Wojtyla's spirituality, something he would confirm first hand in the following years:

> Especially when I saw him pray not only did I see, but understood that he was a man of God. That was my fundamental impression; a man who lives with God, even more, lives *in* God.

Karol Wojtyla's friendship and affection for Cardinal Ratzinger made possible that, after his election, John Paul II called him to Rome on several occasions, until in 1982 he named him prefect of the Congregation for the Doctrine of the Faith. His collaboration would last until the day of his death. Their friendship and closeness though have transcended the barrier of physical death.

John Paul II accompanied his successor step by step throughout his pontificate's eight difficult years. Benedict XVI has not hidden his awareness of this constant presence from the world.

Speaking before Polish television he recognized that he remained in contact with him, not only through the magisterial texts that he left behind and which they had always discussed together, but also through his being, his memory.

> Through his writings, the Pope is always near; I hear and see him speak, and can remain in continuous dia-

logue with the Holy Father because through these words he is always talking to me. I also know the origin of many of the texts, and the dialogues we had about each one of them. I can continue a dialogue with the Holy Father.

Naturally, this closeness through words is not only with the texts but with the person: beyond the text, I listen to the Pope himself. Whoever goes to be with the Lord is not far away: I feel more strongly that each time a man goes to be with the Lord he becomes even closer to me; thus when I am near the Lord, I am near the Pope, and he then helps me to draw closer to the Lord and to try to enter into an atmosphere of prayer, of love for the Lord and love for the Virgin and I commend myself to their prayers.

There is something very significant in the fact that on many occasions Benedict XVI referred to his predecessor as "the Pope," as if he himself wasn't the Pope but John Paul II. Monsignor Alfred Xuereb, who was Pope Benedict's second secretary, and is actually Pope Francis' now, was witness to this on more than one occasion in his eight year pontificate.

Monsignor Xuereb recalls the manner in which Pope Benedict followed the beatification process step by step, and the joy that he did not hide when he was given confirmation that the miracle had been approved. "He spoke about this a lot at the table, and wanted to share his joy with us." To Monsignor Xuereb, the most telling gesture of the now Pope Emeritus' feelings was the shout with which he announced to the world that John Paul was "Blessed." "I had never heard Pope Benedict shout and, in fact, aside from that moment, he never did it again."

Throughout the twenty-six years that Cardinal Ratzinger collaborated with John Paul II, the now Pope Emeritus matured in the conviction that he was working near a saintly man.

> For twenty-three years, I was able to be near him and venerate him increasingly. His profound spirituality and the richness of his intuitions sustained my service. His example of prayer has always impressed and edified me.

This conviction was reinforced during the Via Crucis that John Paul II lived through during the last months of his life. The then Pope Benedict narrated to Polish television:

> I had my last two encounters with him; the first in the Gemelli Policlinic, around February 5-6; and the second in his room, the day before his death. During the first encounter the Pope was suffering visibly, but was totally lucid and present.
>
> I had gone over for a work meeting because I needed some sort of decision from him. Although suffering, the Holy Father followed everything I said very attentively. He communicated his decision in very few words, gave me his blessing, greeted me in German, and granted me his trust and friendship. It was very moving for me to see how his suffering had him joined to the suffering Lord, how he carried his suffering with and for the Lord, and on the other hand to see how his inner peace and complete lucidity shone through.
>
> The last encounter was the day before his death.

Of course I noticed he was, as could be imagined, in more pain as doctors and friends surrounded him. He was still quite lucid and gave me his blessing. He could not talk that much. To me, his patience in suffering has been a great lesson, above all to see and feel how he was in God's hands, how he abandoned himself to His will. Despite the visible suffering, he was serene because he was in the hands of Divine Love.

The friendship and affection that had bonded them was manifest on April 20, during the funeral Mass that Cardinal Ratzinger had to celebrate by virtue of being the Dean of the College of Cardinals. The world was moved when he, visibly moved, said:

It seems as if he is taking me very strongly by the hand: I see his smiling eyes and listen to his words, which he addresses to me at this very moment: "Don't be afraid!"

Nor has anyone forgotten the last words that he pronounced at the end of the Mass:

We can be assured that our beloved Pope is now by the window in the House of the Father, looking at us and blessing us. Yes, bless us Holy Father.

Year after year throughout the eight years of his pontificate, Benedict XVI remembered his predecessor's death. Each celebration was an opportunity to sketch the features of a sanctity that he had been able to feel first hand. Year after year he shared with the world the direct experience of the virtues he had seen in John Paul II. The strength of his faith is what stood out the most in him. To Benedict XVI, John Paul II was a "rock" of faith.

> Those who had the opportunity to know him closely could somehow feel his simple and firm kind of faith which, in addition to impressing his closest collaborators during his long pontificate, did not cease to extend his beneficial influence throughout the entire Church, in a *crescendo* that reached its peak during the last months and days of his life. A convinced, strong and authentic faith, without fear or compromise that won the hearts of many people, thanks to his apostolic pilgrimages throughout the world among other reasons, and especially to that last trip that was his agony and death.

On many occasions he recalled the manner in which John Paul II had demonstrated his love of Christ throughout his entire life.

He remembered what John Paul II had revealed on the occasion of his pontificate's twenty-fifth anniversary about the moment of his election, when in his heart he had felt the question that Jesus made to Peter: "Do you love me? Do you love me more than these?" John Paul II added that each day he repeated the same dialogue between Jesus and Peter in his heart.

> In spirit I contemplate the resurrected Christ's benevolent gaze. He, aware of my human weakness, encourages me to respond with confidence, like Peter:

"Lord, you know everything; you know that I love you." And then invites me to assume the responsibilities that He Himself had entrusted to me.

According to Benedict XVI, John Paul demonstrated his love of Christ, which was his dominant force, looking to reach out to everyone, with his heart wide open and a disposition to forgive, without reservation and without sparing any efforts.

Thanks to his profound rooting in Christ, he has been able to carry a weight that goes beyond pure human strength; to be a shepherd of Christ's flock, of His universal Church.

Cardinal Ratzinger witnessed the manner in which John Paul II prepared himself throughout his life, especially in the last few years, for his encounter with Jesus. During the years that he was at his side, he was most impressed by the manner in which John Paul II prayed, and lost himself in God.

While celebrating the third anniversary of his death, Pope Benedict indicated being convinced that among the "human and supernatural qualities" that John Paul II possessed, he had an "exceptional and mystical spiritual sensibility."

It was enough to observe him when he prayed: he literally submerged himself in God and it seemed that in those moments, everything else was alien to him. During Eucharistic celebrations he was focused on the mystery he was fulfilling, with a notable capacity to capture the essence of God's word in the course of history, in the profound level of God's plan. As he repeated frequently, the Holy Mass was to him the center of each day and his entire life. The Eucharist's "Holy and Living" reality gave him spiritual energy to guide God's people through the path of history.

In the last phase of his earthly life, his mysticism was even more evident. To mark the second anniversary of his death he expressed:

> During the long periods of prayer in his private chapel, he talked to Him, totally abandoning himself to His will, and entrusting himself to Mary, repeating *Totus tuus.*
>
> Like his Divine Master, he lived his agony in prayer. During the last day of his life, the eve of Divine Mercy Sunday, he asked that precisely the Gospel of John be read to him. With assistance from the people who accompanied him, he wanted to participate in all the daily prayers, the Liturgy of the Hours, do the worship and meditation. He died praying. He truly fell asleep in the Lord.

On many occasions, Pope Benedict expressed his conviction that his predecessor's pontificate was a total answer to God's calling, which could not be expressed without participating in Jesus' sufferings and death.

He never ceased to share his testimony about the central role that the cross played in the Polish Pope's life. During his pontificate's 25th anniversary, Cardinal Ratzinger in his role of Dean addressed him with a congratulatory message. It was the year 2003 and the cross, two years from his death, was already very visible.

In your life, the "cross" expression is not just a word. You have allowed yourself to be hurt by it in body and soul. Just like St. Paul, and through the body of Christ that is the Church, you also endure your sufferings in order to complete what still remains of Christ's.

On the day of John Paul II's funeral, his words moved the world.

The Holy Father has been a priest until the very end, because he has given his life to God for His sheep and for the entire human family, as a daily offering in the service of the Church and above all, through the difficult tribulations of the last few months. That is how he became one with Christ, the Good Shepherd who loves His sheep.

We all know that our Pope did not want to save his life, to keep it for himself; he wanted, until the last moment, to give himself for Christ and also for us, without reservation.

A year later, to mark the celebration the first anniversary of his death, Pope Benedict used the word "holocaust" to describe the manner in which John Paul II had surrendered his life to God and mankind.

The word "holocaust" makes reference to the sacrifice in which the victim was burned completely, and consumed by fire; therefore it was a sign of a total offering to God. This biblical expression makes us think about John Paul II's mission, who made his existence an offering to God and the Church, and lived his priesthood's sacrificial dimension especially in the celebration of the Eucharist.

During the second anniversary of his death, Pope Benedict once again spoke about the meaning of the cross in his predecessor's life.

> As we know, the fertility of that testimony relies on the cross. The word "cross" was not just a word in Karol Wojtyla's life. He experienced pain and death since his childhood and adolescence. As a priest and bishop, and above all as supreme pontiff, he took the resurrected Christ's call to Peter along the shore of Lake Galilee: "Follow me. You follow me," very seriously. Especially during the slow but implacable progress of the disease which gradually stripped him of everything, his existence was transformed into a complete offering to Christ, a living proclamation of His Passion, with a faithful hope in the resurrection.

Three years after his death, his successor re-emphasized John Paul II's participation in the cross of Christ.

> That affirmation is true: if we have died with Him we will also live with Him; if we remain firm, we will also reign with Him.

Since his childhood, Karol Wojtyla had experienced the truth of those words, finding the cross along the way, in his family and in his own town. He soon decided to carry it along with Jesus, following in His footsteps. He wanted to be His faithful servant until embracing the call to become a priest as a gift and commitment of a lifetime. He lived with Him, and with Him he also wanted to die.

Cardinal Joseph Ratzinger lived John Paul II's last days of life close by the side of him who, perhaps prophetically, had given him the job of preparing the meditations for what would be the last Via Crucis in his life.

The Cardinal shook the Church with these meditations in which he reported that the Church looked like a ship that was sinking under the weight of its filth.

John Paul II could not participate in the Via Crucis at the Colosseum. He had to follow the route of the fourteen stations from his chapel where a television set had been placed. That evening the world was struck by the image of the Pope, his back turned, embracing the cross of Christ. This is perhaps the most emblematic image of his pontificate.

Cardinal Ratzinger was also struck by this image and four years later, while presiding at the Mass to mark the fourth anniversary of his predecessor's death, he recalled those days:

> We cannot forget that last and silent testimony of love for Jesus. Nor can we forget that eloquent scene of human suffering and faith which on that last Good Friday showed to the faithful and the world the secret of a life that was entirely Christian. His "Do not be afraid!" was not supported by human strength or by successes achieved, but only on the word of God, on the cross and Christ's resurrection.
>
> This abandonment in Christ was revealed in a way that was more and more evident as he was stripped of everything, even the word itself at the end. As it happened to Jesus, also to John Paul II when in the

end, words gave way to extreme sacrifice, the gift of himself. And death was the seal of an existence totally surrendered to Christ, configured in Him even physically by the features of suffering and trusted abandonment to the arms of our Heavenly Father. As those who were near him testified, his last words were: "Let me go to the Father"; that is how a life totally oriented to know and contemplate the Lord's face ended.

A year later he described John Paul II's life and mission, marked by a generous surrender without reservations, without measure, without calculations, as follows:

> What moved him was his love of Christ, to whom he had consecrated his life, an over abundant and unconditional love. And precisely because he became increasingly closer to God through love, he could make himself a traveling companion for the man of today, extending the perfume of God's love throughout the world. Whoever experienced the joy of knowing and frequenting his presence could feel how alive the certainty of "contemplating the Lord's goodness in the land of the living" was, a certainty that accompanied him throughout his entire life and that manifested itself during the last period of his earthly pilgrimage in a special way. In fact, his progressive physical weakness never made a dent on his immovable faith, his luminous hope, nor his fervent charity. He allowed himself to be consumed by Christ, by the Church, by the entire world. His was a suffering lived for love and with love, until the end.

When responding to a question on Polish television about what had been the most relevant aspect of John Paul II's pontificate, Pope Benedict XVI made a distinction between the pontificate as seen from outside, towards the world, and the pontificate as seen from inside, towards the Church.

> In respect to the world, I think that through his speeches, his person, his presence, his capacity to convince, the Holy Father generated a new sensibility towards moral values, and the importance of religion in the world. This made possible a new opening, a new sensibility towards religious problems, a need for mankind's religious dimension, and above all, the unimaginable growth and importance of the Bishop of Rome. Despite their differences and lack of recognition for Peter's successor, all Christians have recognized that he is Christianity's spokesperson.
>
> Worldwide, no one other than he could speak on Christianity's behalf and give voice and strength in the world today to Christian reality. Even for non-Christians and other religions alike, he was the spokesperson for humanity's great values.
>
> I must also mention that he was able to create a climate of dialogue among the great religions, a sense of responsibility that we all have towards the world, making clear that violence is incompatible with all religions and that together we must search for a path to peace, in a common responsibility before humankind.

With respect to the life of the Church, Benedict XVI said that what was most notable was that he knew how to instill enthusiasm for Christ in young people, something totally innovative if one thinks about the youth movements of 1968 and the seventies.

> For young people to become enthusiastic about Christ and the Church, and also with difficult values could only be achieved by a personality with that charisma: only he could mobilize the young people of the world for God's cause and Christ's love, like he did.

Pope Benedict also affirmed that John Paul II generated a new love for the Eucharist in the Church, gave Divine Mercy a new significance, and greatly increased love for the Virgin Mary.

In fact, Cardinal Ratzinger witnessed the manner in which John Paul II's love for Christ passed through Mary. According to Pope Benedict, his Marian vocation was one of the most characteristic features of his predecessor's spirituality. It was no coincidence that he chose May 1, 2011, the month of the Virgin Mary, to beatify him.

After taking on the role of being the first Pope to have the fortune of beatifying his immediate predecessor, Benedict XVI explained John Paul II's love for Mary in this way:

> Karol Wojtyla participated in the Second Vatican Council, first as an auxiliary bishop and later as Archbishop of Cracow, and knew that to have dedicated the last chapter of the document to Mary signified to place the Mother of the Redeemer as image and model of sanctity for all Christians and the entire Church.
>
> This theological vision is the one that Blessed John

Paul II discovered as a youth, and later kept and deep-ened during his entire life. It is a vision that is sum-marized in the biblical icon of Christ on the cross and Mary, his mother, at his feet. An icon that is found in the Gospel of John (19:25-27) and that was sum-marized in Karol Wojtyla's episcopal, and later papal, shield: a golden cross, the letter M below to the right, and the motto: *Totus tuus*, which corresponds to St. Louis Mary Grignion de Montfort's famous expres-sion, in which Karol Wojtyla found a fundamental principle for his life: *Totus tuus ego sum et omnia mea tua sunt. Accipio Te in mea Omnia. Praebe mihi cor tuum, Maria* ("I am all yours and everything I possess is yours. You are my all, O Mary. Lend me your heart.")

That John Paul II returned to the House of the Father on the eve of the Feast of Divine Mercy that he himself had insti-tuted very strongly impressed all of those who lived the last days of his life at his side, among them Cardinal Ratzinger. This sentiment was reflected in the unforgettable homily that he pro-nounced during his funeral. Cardinal Ratzinger affirmed that John Paul II had interpreted the paschal mystery as a mystery of Divine Providence.

On the third anniversary of his death, Pope Benedict re-called that John Paul II himself used to say that God's mercy is one of the keys to the reading of his privileged pontificate. "He wanted the message of God's merciful love to reach all mankind, and he exhorted the faithful to be its promoters."

Pope Benedict explained that John Paul II had personally known and lived the enormous tragedies of the twentieth cen-tury, and for a long time wondered what could stop the tide of evil. He reached the conclusion that the only possible answer was God's love:

> In effect, only Divine Mercy can put a limit to evil; only the love of our Almighty God can defeat the prepotency of the wicked and the destructive power of selfishness and hatred. For this reason, and during his last visit to Poland, upon returning to the land of his birth, he said: "Aside from God's mercy, there is no other source of hope."

During the two decades that he collaborated with him, Cardinal Ratzinger matured in the conviction that John Paul II was a man chosen by God. The message that he dedicated on the occasion of his pontificate's twenty-fifth anniversary, is one of the most eloquent testimonies of this certainty.

> Not only have you traveled the world tirelessly to take the Gospel of the love of God Incarnate in Jesus Christ to mankind, beyond all geographic confines; you have also bridged the continents of the spirit, often distant and opposed to each other, to bring together those who were far apart, to reconcile those who were separated, and to give space in the world to the peace of Christ.
>
> You have addressed young and old, rich and poor, the powerful and the humble and, following Christ's example, have always demonstrated a special love for the poor and the defenseless, taking a spark of God's truth and love to all of them. Fearlessly, you have announced God's will, even there where it comes in

conflict with what mankind thinks and wants. Like the Apostle St. Paul, you can say that you have not attempted to flatter with words, have never sought any honors from men, but have cared for your children like a mother. Like St. Paul, you, too, were fond of men and wanted to make them participants not only of the Gospel, but also of your own life. You accepted criticism and insults, responding in turn with gratitude and love, thus bringing down the walls of hatred and hostility. Today we can see how you have surrendered your whole being to the service of the Gospel, and have been totally exhausted in the process.

Throughout his pontificate, Pope Benedict heard the voice of his predecessor whispering in his ears, repeating: "Don't be afraid." On several occasions he recalled that those words became a kind of motto on the lips of John Paul II.

He repeated it many times to both the Church and to all humanity on the way to the year 2000, and also later during that historical milestone and after at the dawn of the third millennium. He always pronounced it with inflexible strength, first brandishing the pastoral staff that culminates with the cross and later, when his physical energies were declining, almost clinging to it, until that last Good Friday in which he participated in the Via Crucis from his private chapel, embracing the cross in his arms.

During difficult times Pope Benedict recalled the invitation to hope that also became a motto during his predecessor's pontificate. Two years after his death he said:

His repeated invitations to advance without fear on the path faithful to the Gospel in order to be Christ's heralds and witnesses in the third millennium, resounds in our soul.

His incessant exhortations to cooperate generously in the realization of a more just and integral humanity, to be artificers of peace and builders of hope, also come to mind. That our gaze always be fixed on Christ, the same yesterday, today and always, who firmly guides His Church.

To celebrate the fourth anniversary of his death, Pope Benedict once again spoke about the hope that John Paul II had awakened in the world, especially among the new generations, to whom he gave the World Youth Days, an initiative without precedent in the life of the Church.

It is true! John Paul II managed to communicate a great burst of hope, founded on faith in Jesus Christ, who "is the same yesterday, today and always," as he recited the motto of the Great Jubilee of the Year 2000. As an affectionate father and attentive educator, he pointed out sure and firm points of reference that are indispensable for all, especially for young people. And in the moment of his agony and death, this new generation wanted to manifest that it had understood his teachings, gathering silently in prayer in St. Peter's Square and many other places throughout the world.

The young people felt that his disappearance would constitute a loss: "their" Pope, whom they considered "their father" in the faith, was dying. At the same time they realized that he had left them his courage and the coherence of his testimony as his legacy. Had he not stressed many times the need for a radical adherence to the Gospel, exhorting both adults and young people to take this common educational responsibility seriously? He confessed that he himself had wanted to recover some of his own eagerness.

To celebrate the fourth anniversary of his death, Pope Benedict said he was prepared to carry very high the flame of faith, hope and love that John Paul II had lit in the world.

It is the flame that John Paul II has left us as a legacy. He has handed it over to me as his successor; and this afternoon I hand it over ideally, one more time, to you youths of Rome in a special way, so that you may continue to be sentinels of the morning, vigilant and joyful in this the dawn of the third millennium. Respond generously to Christ's calling!

Almost at the beginning of his pontificate, Pope Benedict traveled to Cologne to participate in the World Youth Day that John Paul II had organized, even knowing that he would probably not be present. When announcing it, at the end of the encounter in Toronto, Canada, John Paul II told the young people: "Christ awaits you in Cologne." On previous occasions he always said that he awaited them at what would be their next encounter.

Throughout his pontificate, Pope Benedict repeatedly exalted the legacy that John Paul II had left to him, the Church, and the world. To celebrate the first anniversary of his death, one year prior to his beatification, he described him as follows:

> During his long pontificate, he was prodigal in proclaiming the right with firmness, without weakness or hesitation, especially when he had to confront resistance, obstacles and rejections. He knew that the Lord was holding him by the hand, and this enabled him to exercise a fertile ministry.

The day of John Paul II's beatification, and with words full of emotion, Pope Benedict summarized the true meaning of his predecessor's pontificate.

> "Do not be afraid! Open, open wide the doors to Christ!" What the newly-elected Pope asked of everyone, he was himself the first to do: society, culture, political and economic systems he opened up to Christ, turning back with the strength of a titan – a strength which came to him from God – a tide which appeared irreversible. By his witness of faith, love, and apostolic courage, accompanied by great human charisma, this exemplary son of Poland helped believers throughout the world not to be afraid to be called Christian, to belong to the Church, to speak of the Gospel. In a word: he helped us not to fear the truth, because truth is the guarantee of liberty. To put it even more succinctly: he gave us the strength to believe in Christ, because Christ is *Redemptor hominis*, the Redeemer of man. This was the theme of his first encyclical, and the thread which runs through all the others.

His conviction that John Paul II had been a holy man led him to accept after his election, a proposal from various Cardinals who during the 2005 Conclave meetings had requested the immediate opening of the cause for his beatification, taking into account the chants *Santo Subito* that were heard in St. Peter's Square on the day of his funeral.

Pope Benedict decided to dispense the five year period that must pass after the death of a candidate to the altars, and in May 2005, one month after his election, gave his approval to the opening of the cause for John Paul II's beatification.

By the second anniversary of John Paul II's death, the diocesan phase of the process had already closed. On that occasion Pope Benedict spoke about his predecessor who at that moment was already a servant of God.

> Servant of God is what he was, and we now call him as such in the Church. Servant of God is a title particularly appropriate for him. The Lord called him to His service through the path of priesthood, and gradually opened wider horizons for him: from his diocese to the universal Church. This universal dimension reached its maximum extension at the moment of his death, an event that the entire world lived, with a participation never seen before in history.

To Pope Benedict, after his death John Paul II was always his intercessor in Heaven. His secretary, Monsignor Georg Ganswein, recognized that John Paul II was probably the person whom Benedict XVI appreciated the most. His second secretary, Monsignor Alfred Xuereb, holds the personal conviction that in the months that preceded the difficult, and historic, decision to resign the papacy, Pope Benedict invoked the help of his predecessor, who had made a decision contrary to the one he was preparing to make. Probably, with his help, he understood that both had decided to do the same, in other words, listen to what God was telling them, and do what God was asking them to do.

We owe Benedict XVI the most lyrical pages written about John Paul II after his death. His words about the perfume of his sanctity that invaded the world still resonate.

> The Pope's perfume of faith, hope, and charity filled his home, St. Peter's Square, the Church, and spread throughout the world. For those who believe, what transpired after his death was an effect from that "perfume" which reached everyone, near and afar, and attracted them to a man whom God had progressively configured with his Christ.

# 9 John Paul II and Francis

To Pope Francis, saints are neither supermen nor perfect people. They are like us; people who, before achieving sainthood, had lived a normal life, with joys, sufferings, fatigue and hopes.

When he celebrated the Feast of All Saints as Pope, Francis asked himself what makes the difference in a saint. He went on to explain that upon knowing God's love, "saints have followed Him with all their hearts, without conditions or hypocrisies; they have dedicated their lives to the service of others, endured suffering and tribulations without hatred, and responded to evil with good will, spreading peace and joy."

To Pope Francis, saints are people who have understood that hatred comes from the devil; therefore they have distanced themselves from him. "Saints are men and women," he commented, "that have joy in their hearts and transmit it to others."

He summarized sainthood this way: "Never hate, be at the service of others, especially the neediest, pray, and be joyful. This is the road to sainthood."

Borrowing one of John Paul II's convictions, he also explained that to be a saint is not the privilege of a few, as if someone had received a great inheritance. We can all aspire to sainthood and we can all achieve it. We are all called to sainthood, because it is not about doing extraordinary things, but allowing God to work in our lives.

According to Pope Francis, saints are people with simple and humble hearts who do not presume to be just, do not judge others, know how to suffer with those who suffer, rejoice with others' joy, are not violent but merciful, and try to be architects of reconciliation and peace.

Three and a half months after having been elected, Pope Francis received the documentation relative to Floribeth Mora Diaz's miraculous healing from the hands of Cardinal Angelo Amato, Prefect of the Congregation for the Causes of Saints. The miracle had already been approved by the Congregation. On that day, July 5, 2013, the Pope signed the decree of the miracle, thus paving the way for John Paul II's canonization.

As it is customarily done in a cause for canonization, the Pope sent a letter to all the Cardinals throughout the world asking whether or not they were in agreement with his decision to canonize both John Paul II and John XXIII. In the case of John XXIII, and despite having received testimonies of several graces received or alleged miracles having occurred, Pope Francis decided that his fame for sanctity could result in avoiding the study and approval of any of them. The Cardinals' positive response was unanimous.

> Several weeks later, on board the plane that returned him to Rome from Brazil after having celebrated World Youth Day, and during a one hour and twenty minute encounter with the journalists who accompanied him, Pope Francis in response to my question, went on to explain why he had decided to canonize John XXIII and John Paul II: "Regarding John

Paul II, I would say he was 'the great missionary of the Church': he was a missionary, a man who carried the Gospel everywhere, as you know better than I. How many trips did he make? But he went! He felt this fire of carrying forth the Word of the Lord. He was like Paul, like St. Paul, he was such a man; for me this is something great. And to canonize them both together will be, I believe, a message for the Church: these two were wonderful, both of them."

*Valentina Alazraki*

According to Professor Guzman Carriquiry, the first lay secretary of the Pontifical Commission for Latin America, a friend of Cardinal Bergoglio for several decades and collaborator to five Popes, Pope Francis shares the missionary eagerness with John Paul II. With his pilgrimages, the Polish Pope put Pope Paul VI's *Evangelii Nuntiandi* into practice, thus launching a new evangelization. Pope Francis, heir to the end of John Paul II's complex pontificate and the eight difficult years of Benedict XVI's, has interpreted mission differently: the mission begins at home, in the transformation of hearts and minds, extending towards the existential, material, and religious peripheries.

John Paul II did not like to occupy himself with the curia, as he did not want to be tied down by those mechanisms. This is why he conceived the mission as a constant pilgrimage towards the world. Pope Francis, who in reality was never a great traveler, now has to dedicate himself to putting his house in order, but his missionary spirit is the same.

The frontiers change, but not the impetus. According to Professor Carriquiry, there is another nuance that differentiates his vision of the mission. Through his travels, John Paul II swept through the local episcopates and somehow made up for a certain passivity that enabled his evangelical dynamism and overwhelming missionary enthusiasm to carry them along. Pope Francis on the other hand, in his eagerness to decentralize and expand collegiality, wants the episcopates to be the protagonists of that missionary fervor, and not hide behind the leadership of a charismatic Pope.

Like Pope Francis, while feeling deeply his being bishop of Rome, John Paul II also felt the requirement to go to the peripheries. From his first pilgrimage to Mexico, he understood that he could not only dedicate himself to the Diocese of Rome, but had to demonstrate his proximity to the Universal Church; he had to go to the material, existential, and even juridical peripheries, as explained by Cardinal Lozano Barragan, who collaborated with him throughout his entire pontificate. "To go to Mexico, a country with which the Vatican had no diplomatic relations, meant to go towards a juridical periphery without fear."

His desire was to take Christ to the world's peripheries, to return the reasons for hope to humankind. We saw him near lepers in Brazil and Africa; the sick from AIDS in the United States; Mother Teresa's dying in Calcutta; the favelas and neighborhoods of misery in the five continents; the drug addicts, the marginalized, the detained, the disabled, the remnants of society.

In his first apostolic exhortation *The Joy of the Gospel*, Pope Francis recalled that John Paul II invited us to recognize that "it is necessary to keep interest in the Gospel message alive" in those who are distant from Christ, because "this is the overriding task of the Church."

According to Monsignor Alfred Xuereb, who was prelate of the Antechamber during the last years of John Paul II's pontificate, and who is now Pope Francis' secretary, Pope Francis shares a tireless pastoral care with John Paul II. "They are two men of God, two pastors whose mission is their service to the Church, who commit themselves to take the Gospel to all, to make God's Kingdom more alive in the world each day."

In the election of John Paul II – the first non-Italian Pope to be elected in the last five hundred years – and his decision to initiate his worldwide mission in Latin America, a continent that stole his heart, followed by the election of a German Pope who represented the highest European figure within the Church and his unexpected resignation, and finally the election of a Latin American Pope, Professor Guzman Carriquiry saw a thread woven by Providence. To him, it is no coincidence that of John Paul II's 104 trips throughout the world, he visited twenty-two Latin American countries.

> In his spiritual and missionary geography, Latin America exerted an extraordinary attraction to the Polish Pope: John Paul II was aware of a change in the geo-religious landscape; he knew that the Catholic heart throbbed in Latin America, and not in Old Europe, already shaken by a religious and moral crisis.

According to Professor Carriquiry, John Paul II, with whom he collaborated very closely, was aware that 42% of the world's Catholics lived in what he qualified as the "continent of hope." John Paul II sensed that while Europe was, according to many points of view, going through a decline, the Church in Latin America was alive.

In the beginning of his pontificate, Pope Benedict XVI also decided to travel to Latin America to participate in the Fifth Conference of the Latin American Episcopate that took place in Aparecida, Brazil. While on board the plane that took him to Brazil, and in response to a question that sounded more like criticism of his alleged Eurocentrism, he recognized that at least in part, and a fundamental one, the destiny of the Catholic Church passed through Latin America. Gestures and prophetic words paved the way for the election of Pope Francis.

There are bonds that are not so visible which unite these three Popes, protagonists of the most collaborative canonization in the history of the Church.

The first act in John Paul II's international stage was to inaugurate the Third Latin American Episcopal Conference in Puebla, Mexico in 1979. Pope Benedict inaugurated the Fifth in Aparecida, Brazil, but on that occasion the key man, the editor of the final document was Cardinal Bergoglio. According to Professor Guzman Carriquiry, there is a thread that binds John Paul II with Pope Francis that passes through the Latin American Bishops' Conference in Puebla, Mexico, in which the Polish Pope drafted the directives for his pontificate as it related to social justice, the mission of the Church, and the conference in Aparecida in which Bergoglio played a significant role.

> There is a very close link between these meetings, which have been fundamental to the self-awareness of the Latin American Church. At the time, Bergoglio fully recognized himself in the Puebla document, which in some way was the great translation of Pope Paul VI's *Evangelii Nuntiandi*, which is the papal document of the last fifty years that Pope Francis appreciates the most.

According to one of the men closest to the Pope, both John Paul II and now Pope Francis stand out on this parallel road like "two pastors with a profound sense of the people." Perhaps John Paul II stands out as a vigorous leader, whereas Pope Francis prefers to present himself to the world as a father and brother; both have the same strong rapport with the people, possess a natural sympathy, and enjoy being near the people; both are pastors close to their people. "Like Benedict XVI, both live their lives in an encounter with Christ," he affirms.

During his meeting with journalists on board the plane returning him from the World Youth Day that took place in Brazil, and while speaking about the merciful outlook that the Church must show in the difficult situations of our day, Pope Francis once again referred to John Paul II.

> I believe that this is the season of mercy. This new era we have entered, and the many problems in the Church – like the poor witness given by some priests, problems of corruption in the Church, the problem of clericalism for example – have left so many people hurt, left so much hurt. The Church is a mother; she has to go out to heal those who are hurting, with mercy. If the Lord never tires of forgiving, we have no other choice than this: first of all, to care for those who are hurting. The Church is a mother, and she must travel this path of mercy. And find a form of mercy for all. When the prodigal son returned home, I don't think his father told him: "You, sit down and listen: what did you do with the money?" No! He celebrated! Then, perhaps, when the son was ready to speak, he spoke. The Church has to do this, when

there is someone… not only wait for them, but go out and find them! That is what mercy is. And I believe that this is a *kairos*: this time is a *kairos* of mercy. But John Paul II had the first intuition of this, when he began with Faustina Kowalska, the Divine Mercy… He had something, he had intuited that this was a need in our time.

One of the fundamental aspects of John Paul II's mission was undoubtedly his trust in God's mercy. To him, the author of the encyclical *Dives in misericordia* dedicated to mercy and promoter of the Faustina Kowalska cult; it was about a spontaneous impulse born from his heart, from the experiences lived in contact with the horrors of the twentieth century, with Nazism and Communism, which provoked desperation, annihilation, and the obliteration of human dignity. To him, the Christian response was trust in God's mercy. Like Pope Francis, John Paul II was convinced that God is always on the side of man, of the sinner, the unhappy, and the victims of injustice. On the one hand he surrendered to God's mercy, and on the other, he felt a profound responsibility towards his brothers and sisters, and this made him demonstrate this mercy by loving God and all human beings.

Pope Francis never tires of speaking about this mercy and forgiveness. Almost daily, he repeats that God always forgives, and that it is man who tires of asking forgiveness.

In a letter not made known at that time, to terrorist Ali Agca, who shot him on May 13, 1981, John Paul II wrote that "the act of forgiveness is the first and fundamental condition for us men not to be divided against each other as enemies." According to Cardinal Angelo Amato, Prefect for the Congregation for the Causes of Saints, mercy unites John Paul II and Pope Francis. He went on to explain:

> Mercy includes charity, Jesus' only commandment. Mercy is most important today because it signifies forgiveness, to have the courage to reconcile with others, not to speak ill of others, and to do good concretely. I believe that mercy is truly John Paul II's insignia. Both he and Pope Francis are men of great mercy, charity, and peace.

According to him, with this canonization Pope Francis recognizes John XXIII and John Paul II as the precursors of his pontificate.

> Pope Francis follows in John XXIII's footsteps in terms of his goodness, and John Paul II's in terms of his mercy. He unites these two witnesses with simplicity, and transforms them by the way in which he approaches the faithful, his constant smile, and his embrace of the world. Pope Francis rejoices in being able to elevate to the altars these two figures that the world appreciates and has never forgotten.

Another theme that unites John Paul II and Pope Francis is their preferential option for the poor. In his apostolic exhortation *The Joy of the Gospel*, Pope Francis recalled that John Paul II affirmed this during the Mass for the Evangelization of Peoples in the Dominican Republic in 1984.

To the Church, the preferential option for the poor is a theological category before it is a cultural, sociological, political or philosophical one. "God grants them," John Paul II said, "his first mercy."

Pope Francis also recalled that in his encyclical *Sollicitudo Rei Socialis*, written in 1987, Pope John Paul II, inspired by this preference, wrote that the Church opted for the poor understood as "a special form of primacy in the exercise of Christian charity."

Monsignor Alfred Xuereb considers that, like John Paul II, Pope Francis pays special attention to the most needy and most marginalized people. According to him, the simplest of people feel valued and important to him, and therefore to God. "He makes them feel that they play a valuable role in God's eyes, that they are unique, useful and with an extraordinary dignity."

Upon returning to Brazil, on board the aircraft the Pope announced to the journalists that he would carry out the double canonization probably on April 27, Divine Mercy Sunday, which feast was instituted precisely by John Paul II after canonizing Faustina Kowalska, the Polish sister and promoter of the Divine Mercy cult, in 2000.

In effect, on September 30, 2013, the Pope held a consistory, a solemn meeting of Roman Catholic cardinals convoked and presided over by the Pope, in which he announced that the double canonization would indeed take place on that date. He would have preferred to celebrate it on December 8, the date on which the Second Vatican Council was adjourned and the Feast of the Immaculate Conception, but Cardinal Dziwisz, John Paul II's former secretary and Archbishop of Cracow, commented that the cold and snow would have made travel difficult for the Polish faithful of scarce resources who could not afford air travel. Cold temperatures would have also represented a problem for those who might decide to camp out and wait for the ceremony. Pope Francis immediately understood these arguments and postponed the double canonization until the following spring.

Cardinal Angelo Amato witnessed the joy that it represented to Pope Francis to be able to announce his decision to canonize two of his predecessors. He commented that John XXIII was to Pope Francis the good Pope who, by convoking Vatican Council II, made it possible for the Church to live a new springtime. John Paul II put the Council's teaching into practice, and now he was harvesting the legacy of both. To Pope Francis, John XXIII and John Paul II represent two of the Church's columns. According to Cardinal Amato, with this canonization, Pope Francis recognizes the extraordinary way in which John Paul II lived faith, hope and charity, especially his faith because he lived and strengthened it in the midst of many difficulties, including persecution, oppression by the communist regime, and the Nazi occupation. Pope Francis recognized that John Paul II took the Gospel to all the ends of the earth. He went to all the continents, and courageously established a dialogue with all. With this canonization, Pope Francis also recognized his extraordinary strength. Cardinal Amato stated:

> When on May 13, 1981, he was wounded by Ali Agca, John Paul II was on the threshold of Paradise, but Providence made him back up and returned him to life because he still had many things to do. From that moment on, he spent his entire life paying homage to Divine Providence, announcing the Gospel, spreading love for Mary, the saints and martyrs, because he was convinced that the 20th century would be the century of martyrs.

Jorge Mario Bergoglio and John Paul II's relationship began twenty-one years before Pope Francis was elected as Pope Benedict XVI's successor.

When Argentinian journalist Elisabetta Pique (author of the well documented book *Life and Revolution* and a good friend of Cardinal Bergoglio who baptized both of her children whom, because of her love for John Paul II, she named Juan Pablo [Juanpi], and Carolina) went to the curia in Buenos Aires to see Cardinal Bergoglio, her attention was always drawn to a picture that was, and still is, on a table in the hallway that led to his office, on which you could see John Paul II drinking "maté" on a plane, perhaps the one that took him to Buenos Aires on one of his two trips to Argentina. She nevertheless recognizes that there was never a great personal relationship between John Paul II and Francis, beyond the importance that the first had on the destiny of the second.

> When John Paul II was elected Pope in October of 1978, Bergoglio was still Provincial of Argentina's Jesuits, a position he continued to occupy until July 31, 1979. Nevertheless, both shared a common vision against attempts to mix Catholic theology with Marxism or to utilize a Marxist social analysis.

As is well known, John Paul II visited Argentina twice: the first time in June 1982, during the Falkland War; the second, in April 1987 for World Youth Day. But Bergoglio, faithful to his low profile and his desire not to expose himself to the spotlight, did not meet with the Polish Pope on either of those two instances.

However, Jorge Bergoglio did run into John Paul II at the CELAM (Latin American Episcopal Conference), which took place in Puebla in 1979, where "he was among those who decidedly opposed those Theology of Liberation schools of thought that used Marxist analysis or were involved in politics, arguing that the Latin American continent needed to reflect its own cultural and religious tradition."

According to Cardinal Javier Lozano Barragan, the Vatican's former Secretary of Health, the only Mexican prelate in the Roman curia for many years and a friend of Cardinal Bergoglio for forty years, it is undeniable that Pope Francis and John Paul II share the same preferential love for the poor, but in both cases it is an evangelical love, centered in Christ and not on ideologies.

> Perhaps this love seems more evident and stronger in Pope Francis, but we must keep in mind that in John Paul II's times, and in the midst of many tensions inside and outside the Church, the Pope had to clearly distinguish what Theology of Liberation truly was. Once the way was clarified and having clearly explained that there was no room for Marxist ideologies or assertions, Pope Francis can speak with more freedom and clarity about a poor Church for the poor.

During those convulsed years after the Second Vatican Council, and on the eve of bloody military dictatorships in the "Southern Cone," Elisabetta Pique recalls that "both as Provincial and then as Dean of the Colegio Maximo de San Miguel, Bergoglio strongly defended John Paul II and the Vatican from attacks coming from within the Church, including Jesuits and the clergy itself."

Around the beginning of the decade of the 80's, due to his qualities as a man of God and a man of government, Bergoglio began to be considered by the Vatican as a bishop candidate. So much so that, thanks to efforts of the Nuncio of that time, Ubaldo Calabresi, and requests from Antonio Quarracino, Archbishop of Buenos Aires, John Paul II appointed him auxiliary bishop of the Argentine capital in June 1992. "To Bergoglio, this meant being rescued from exile in Cordoba, imposed upon him two years earlier by the Jesuit authorities who resented his situation within the Order," Pique said after they had run into each other at the Puebla Conference about the Theology of Liberation.

Five years later, John Paul II appointed Bergoglio coadjutor bishop of Buenos Aires and on February 28, 1988, upon Quarracino's death, he automatically became the Archbishop of Buenos Aires, a springboard to the papacy.

On February 21 of 2001, John Paul II appointed him Cardinal. That same year he designated Bergoglio as assistant to the Synod of bishops to take place in October of that same year. When Cardinal Egan of New York had to leave the synod and return to his Diocese after the tragedy of September 11, Bergoglio succeeded him. And on that occasion, his excellent performance earned him international recognition, and many Cardinals began to consider him as a possible *papabile*, John Paul II's successor.

Guillermo Marco, the Cardinal's spokesperson at that time, told the daily *La Nacion* that the morning of the consistory, he stopped by to pick the Cardinal up from the curial house where he had spent the night. As soon as he saw him dressed with his red Cardinal garb and ready for the ceremony, he asked how they were going to the Vatican. "What do you mean, how?", the Cardinal responded. "By foot!" Upon seeing his amazement, he added: "Relax! In Rome, you can walk around with a banana on your head and no one is going to say anything to you."

The other Cardinals entered the Vatican with large groups of relatives and friends. He had taken two members of his family and his spokesperson.

Another difference to the rest of the new Cardinals was that his red attire was not new. He had asked that the one his predecessor, Cardinal Quarracino, had used be mended.

Shortly before the commencement of the ceremony, Cardinal Bergoglio recalled the words that his father used to tell him: "Greet everyone when you are going up, for they are the same people you will encounter when you are coming down." Who would have told him that twelve years later he would once again walk along that same road to enter the conclave from which he would emerge elected Pope.

Every time he had an opportunity to be received by Pope John Paul II, or to assist at a meeting over which he presided, Cardinal Bergoglio was struck by the great attention John Paul II dedicated to the people he received. During the *ad limina* visit that the Argentine bishops made to the Vatican in 2002, he realized that John Paul II had an extraordinary memory that reflected the interest he felt for his listeners. He noted that he dedicated a great deal of time to his encounters with the bishops. When he assisted at a Mass at which the Pope presided, the manner in which he prepared for the Eucharist drew Cardinal Bergoglio's attention. He had the impression of being before a man of God. The manner in which he knelt, totally lost in God, was very moving.

During the last years of John Paul II's life, Cardinal Bergoglio admired the way in which the Pope did not hide his suffering, and the manner in which he attempted to teach the world how to suffer and die, always displaying equilibrium and serenity. He noticed how heroic the last part of the Pope's life was, and above all, his death, that overwhelmed men and women of all social levels, races or religions; Bergoglio was a witness of his reputation for sanctity which was reflected not only in the "Santo Subito" chants in St. Peter's Square, but also in the pilgrimage of faithful from all over the world to visit his tomb.

Four years after having been appointed Cardinal, Bergoglio was designated to celebrate the Mass of suffrage on the occasion of John Paul II's death. In the Buenos Aires Cathedral, the Archbishop highlighted the Polish Pope's authenticity. In his homily, he outlined the profile of a man of God, of a witness:

> John Paul was simply very coherent,* was never deceitful, never lied, and never practiced chicanery. He communicated with his people with the authenticity of a man of God, with the genuineness of one who every morning spent long hours in adoration, and because he adored God, he allowed himself to be shaped by God's strength. Coherence cannot be bought, and is not studied in any career. It is nurtured in the heart through adoration, with the anointing of service to others, and with rectitude of behavior, without lies, deceit or duplicity.
>
> One day while walking, Jesus said of Nathanael: "Here is a true Israelite, without duplicity." I believe we can say the same about John Paul II, the coherent witness. Because he was coherent he allowed himself to be chiseled by God. He allowed himself to be humbled by God's will. He allowed that obedient attitude of our father Abraham and all who followed him to grow within his soul.
>
> We remember a saintly man who once told us that

---

* Translator's Note: Coherence, coherent, coherently are all words that are difficult to translate into English. They carry the idea of someone's being authentic, genuine, transparent, saintly, holy, true to himself, etc.

this century does not need masters, but witnesses, and the saintly man is a witness. He is a man who puts his flesh on the burner and supports with his flesh, his entire life, and with his transparency everything that he preaches.

This coherent man who out of pure coherence dirtied his hands and saved us from a fratricidal massacre; this coherent individual rejoiced in picking children up in his arms because he believed in affection. This coherent person who more than once had men from the streets, here we call them vagabonds, brought from Risorgimento Square to speak to them and offer them a new situation in life. This coherent person, as soon as he felt healthy, asked for permission to visit the jail to speak with the man who had tried to kill him.

He is a true witness. I finish repeating his words: "What we need in this century are not masters, but witnesses." And in the Incarnation of the Word, Christ is that faithful witness. Today we see in John Paul an imitation of this faithful witness. And we are grateful that he ended his life this way, coherently, that he ended his life being simply that: a faithful witness.

On occasion of the death of John Paul II, Cardinal Bergoglio wrote a testimony for the Italian journalist Stefania Falasca of the magazine 30 *Giorni*. He handed it over to her when he arrived in Rome to participate in the conclave, in which according to several reconstructions, he would have been the most voted for candidate, after Cardinal Joseph Ratzinger. This is his testimony:

I was up in front of them all, on my knees. The group was large; I could see the Holy Father with his back turned, and little by little I became lost in prayer. I was not alone; I was praying before the people of God to whom I belonged, and with all of those who were there, guided by our Pastor.

I became distracted halfway through the prayer, looking at the Pope's figure, his piety, his devotion, they were all a testimony! And time vanished, and I began to imagine the young priest, seminarian, poet, worker, the child from Wadowice, in the same position that he was at that moment, praying one Ave Maria after another. His testimony moved me. I felt that this man, chosen to guide the Church, was following the path towards his Mother in Heaven, a path initiated during his childhood.

And then I understood the impact of the Virgin of Guadalupe's words to Juan Diego: "Do not be afraid. Am I not here who are your Mother?" Then I understood the Virgin's presence in the Pope's life. I have not forgotten that testimony for one instant. Henceforth I have always prayed fifteen mysteries of the rosary every day.

From that moment, the seal of unity between John Paul II and Bergoglio was Mary. His collaborators in Buenos Aires have told that Cardinal Bergoglio always carried a plastic and very simple rosary around his neck, which he has not taken off since he arrived at the Vatican. He continues to pray the rosary several times a day, and he finds peace and rest in this prayer.

Professor Guzman Carriquiry commented:

John Paul II and Francis share the same love for the Marian sanctuaries. To them they are true spiritual capitals of the peoples. Both appreciate and value popular religiosity. John Paul II was the *Totus tuus* Pope, the "All yours" directed to Mary. The first thing that Pope Francis did after being elected Pope was to go to the Basilica of St. Mary Major to pay homage to the Virgin who protects the Romans. Both consecrated the world to the Virgin of Fatima who saved John Paul II's life.

According to Professor Carriquiry, there is one more bond that unites the two Popes. At the beginning of his pontificate, John Paul II asked "The Morenita" to open the hearts of the peoples of Latin America:

> And did she open them. In his first outing, Pope Francis traveled to Brazil and commended his pontificate to the Virgin of Aparecida. In 2016 he will go to Cracow, John Paul II's hometown, to preside over the World Youth Day that he himself conceived, and will surely ask the Black Virgin of Czestochowa to open the hearts of all young people around the world just like the Virgin of Aparecida did.

One Sunday in November 2013, and during the prayer of the *Angelus*, Pope Francis surprised the faithful by presenting a small box from his papal studio at the Apostolic Palace, with a "miraculous" medicine, whose name says everything: "Mercycordine." There was a rosary inside each box, and a "prescription" which explained how to pray it.

This came about as an initiative on the part of several Polish seminarians from Gdansk, devotees of the Divine Mercy. Pope Francis' chaplain, Monsignor Konrad Krajewski, who for many years was John Paul II's Master of Ceremonies, took a box of Mercycordine to the Pope and told him in a very serious tone of voice. "Your doctor recommends this medicine; it is great for the heart." The Pope did not take it seriously until after he opened the box and discovered that the medicine was a rosary. He liked the idea so much that he decided to "advertise" it from the world's most famous window.

According to Francis' Polish chaplain, the Pope laughed when he read the "prescription," where it indicated that the remedy has no "side effects," not even for pregnant women, and that it can be used for preventive purposes "once a day and in case of emergency, as many times as the soul needs it." Prior to praying the *Angelus*, the Pope commented to the faithful that one has to take it because it "provides spiritual help to the soul and helps spread love, forgiveness and fraternity. Those fifty-nine miraculous pills," he said, "are good for the heart, soul and one's whole life."

In 2011, on the occasion of John Paul II's beatification, Cardinal Bergoglio celebrated a thanksgiving Mass in the Buenos Aires Cathedral, at which the country's Polish community whose young people dressed in their typical attire, scout groups, and Polish missionaries, assisted. The Pope highlighted the value of the Polish Pope's phrase, "Do not be afraid."

Before Mass began, a life-sized image of John Paul II was brought into the church by publicist Fernando Pugliese, which excited the faithful who cheered the new "Blessed," encouraged by the Cathedral's rector, Father Alejandro Russo. Afterwards the beatification rite ceremony, presided by Benedict XVI at St. Peter's Square was retransmitted and interrupted several times by the effusive applause from the faithful present, an expression of their devotion for the new "Blessed." The celebration culminated with the veneration of a relic of John Paul II. Having finished the Mass, homage to all apostolic movements created or launched during John Paul II's pontificate was projected on a giant screen.

Hundreds of members of these movements, among them members of the Focolare and of Communion and Liberation, were present.

Accompanied by a large number of priests who concelebrated the Mass with him, Cardinal Bergoglio urged everyone to "follow the 'Blessed's example so that Jesus', the angels' and the phrase of 'Blessed John Paul': 'Don't be afraid' would continue to resonate in our ears and in our hearts, because Jesus' Resurrection is the hope to which we are all called, and therefore we should not allow ourselves to 'fear to be happy'. The courage and solidarity that Christ's Resurrection gives us, and the serenity to be forgiven by the mercy that we find in His wounds, takes away the fear," he stressed.

On the first Sunday after Easter, Pope Francis spoke about Christ's Resurrection, and His invitation to not be afraid because Christ had defeated death:

> All the time that follows the Lord's Resurrection is occupied by Him and His angels to pacify and quiet the hearts, open minds; the angels' Easter greeting is one of hope and courage: "Do not be afraid."
>
> Blessed John Paul II told us repeatedly from the beginning: "Do not be afraid" because he lived contemplating his resurrected Lord. He knew that his Redeemer lived, that His wounds watered His Pas-

tor's heart, and wanted to transmit it with the words: "Do not be afraid." A few days ago, in a beautiful expression, Cracow's Archbishop Cardinal Dziwisz, in reference to that phrase said: "That 'don't be afraid' phrase [used by the Pope], toppled dictatorships." The value and firmness that Christ's Resurrection gives us the serenity of being forgiven by the mercy we find in His wounds, takes the fear away.

May Jesus', the angels' and Blessed John Paul II's phrase "Do not be afraid," continue to resonate in our ears and hearts today, and always. And in response, with our hearts and on our knees, may we say to our resurrected Lord: "My Lord and my God." Amen.

Fifteen days after his election, and in one of his first acts as Pope outside of his official agenda, was to go on April 2nd to the tomb of Blessed John Paul II, in remembrance of the eighth anniversary of his death. There he knelt and prayed for a long time.

Eight months after having been elected, Pope Francis celebrated one of his customary Masses before John Paul II's tomb in St. Sebastian's Chapel and next to Michelangelo's Pietà, for a group of Polish priests and faithful. While commenting on the day's readings, he again spoke about St. Paul, the apostle in whose footsteps John Paul II followed according to Pope Francis.

There are two things to admire in these readings. First of all, Paul's certainty: "No one can separate me from the love of Christ." He loved the Lord very much because he had seen Him, encountered Him, the Lord had changed his life; he loved Him so much that he said that nothing could separate him from Him.

It was precisely this love of the Lord that was the center of Paul's life. Nor could persecutions, sickness, betrayals, everything he lived through or other things that happened in his life, separate him from his love of Christ. His love for Christ was the actual center of his life, his reference point.

Without Christ's love, without living that love, recognizing it, and nourishing ourselves from it, one cannot be Christian. A Christian is one who feels looked at by the Lord with that beautiful smile, loved by the Lord, and loved through to the end.

A Christian feels that his life was saved by the blood of Christ. And this is what love is about, a loving relationship.

That is the first thing I admire. The other thing that draws my attention is Jesus' sadness when He looks at Jerusalem and utters that beautiful phrase: "Oh you Jerusalem, who have not understood love." Contrary to what Paul felt, it didn't understand God's tenderness or His love.

But yes, God loves me, God loves all of us, but that is something abstract, it is something that does not touch my heart, and I fit it into life the best I can. There is no loyalty there. And the cry from Jesus' heart to Jerusalem is this: "Jerusalem, you were not faithful, you did not allow yourself to be loved and have surrendered to so many idols that promised and offered you everything, and then abandoned you." Jesus' heart, the suffering of Jesus' love: A rejected love that has not been accepted.

Let's look at these two figures together: On the

one hand that of Paul, who remains faithful to Jesus' love until the end, from which he finds the strength to continue forward, to endure everything. He feels weak, a sinner, but draws strength from God's love, from that encounter which he had with Jesus Christ. On the other hand, the unfaithful city and people who do not accept Jesus' love, or even worse, who live that love halfway: a little yes, a little no, according to their convenience.

Let's take a look at Paul and his courage which comes from that love, and then let's look at Jesus, who cries over that unfaithful city. Let's look at Paul's fidelity, Jerusalem's infidelity, and Jesus' love in the middle, with His heart that loves us so much. What can we do? We can ask ourselves: Do I look more like Paul, or Jerusalem? Is my love for God as strong as Paul's, or lukewarm like Jerusalem's? May the Lord, through the Blessed John Paul II's intercession, help us answer that question.

❧

On May 1, 2013, and on the occasion of the second anniversary of John Paul II's beatification, I had the privilege of attending a private Mass presided over by Pope Francis in St. Martha's residence at 7:00 A.M. At the end of the Mass which I was able to concelebrate with him in remembrance of the beloved Polish Pope, I gave him a small box with a relic of John Paul II. It contained a small piece of the bloodied cassock that he wore on May 13, 1981 during the attack at St. Peter's Square that nearly cost him his life. No words were needed. Pope Francis took the small box in his hands, closed his eyes and kissed the relic of his predecessor whom he would canonize two months later. To me, that gesture was more valuable than a thousand words, and I cherish that moment as an unforgettable memory that will accompany me forever.

*Monsignor Slawomir Oder*

It was even more significant that Pope Francis had decided to send a relic of John Paul II to Iraq as a messenger of peace. The pilgrim Pope wanted to travel to Ur, Iraq in 2000, to follow in the footsteps of Abraham, the common father of all Christians, Muslims and Jews, but was unable to fulfill his dream. John Paul II had revealed:

> I would like to go to Ur of the Chaldees, today's Tell al-Muqayyar in southern Iraq, the city where according to the biblical narration, Abraham heard God's word, which uprooted him from his land, his people, and in some way from himself, to turn him into an instrument for the plan of salvation, which spanned the future of the people of the covenant, and even all the peoples of the world.

John Paul II could not fulfill his dream because Saddam Hussein informed him that he could not guarantee his safety or that of the faithful who might attend these events. On February 23, 2000, the Pope was forced to make a virtual journey to Iraq, the nation whose invasion three years later he would fight against with the last remnants of strength he had left. From the

Paul VI room, the room connected to St. Peter's Square where the general audiences take place, and via large screens, John Paul II presided over the commemoration of Abraham, "our father in the faith." In the middle of a room located in Mesopotamia to relive the beginning of that history, John Paul II asked God "for peace and harmony among Jews, Christians, and Muslims."

Four months before his canonization, and with Pope Francis' blessing, the pilgrim Pope fulfilled his dream. In December, 2013, Monsignor Liberano Andreatta, representing the Roman Society for Pilgrimages, decided to make a prophetic gesture and convert John Paul II into Pope Francis' peace messenger. For the latter he took a life-size bronze statue of the Polish Pope away from the Vatican as a pilgrim of peace which would remain in the Chaldean Cathedral of Ur; a reliquary with a relic from the bloodied cassock that John Paul II wore at the time of the attack on May 13, 1981 for Baghdad's Catholic Cathedral; a procession icon for the Armenian Cathedral; and a peace lamp for the Latin Cathedral, which John Paul II had blessed on February 11, 2001 on the occasion of the World Day of the Sick.

With great emotion Pope Francis kissed the golden brass reliquary, which bears his papal coat and that of John Paul II. To him he entrusted the peace mission that he so much advocates. Both the statue and reliquary crossed Iraq until arriving in Baghdad and Ur as Pope Francis' special peace emissary, therefore fulfilling John Paul II's trip number 105, perhaps the first with which he had wanted to begin, to carry the message of peace and reconciliation to the land in which the history of salvation began, never imagining he would fulfill it representing the Pope who had come from the end of the world and who would make him a saint.